**Date Due**

# Fugue and Invention
## IN THEORY AND PRACTICE

# Fugue and Invention

## IN THEORY AND PRACTICE

By
### John W. Verrall
School of Music
University of Washington

PACIFIC BOOKS, Publishers
Palo Alto, California

# Preface

This book does not pretend to be a history of the fugue. Indeed, it is not essentially historical in its presentation of the techniques the great fugal writers used. It is rather a textbook intended to guide the student into the art of composing and analyzing fugues. To this has been appended a study of invention, since the contrapuntal devices of fugue and invention are related and mutually beneficial.

The plan used in presenting the material in this book is quite simple. First, a given aspect of the fugue or invention is defined and described, i.e., presented in its theoretical aspects. Then it is exemplified by generous quotations from the works of various composers and these examples are explained. Finally, a series of practical exercises in composition and analysis is presented at the end of each chapter.

In a special appendix entitled "Suggested Readings," a bibliography of famous writings on various aspects of the fugue and invention is included. These readings are sufficiently described to enable them to serve as supplemental reading and study of specific techniques.

The author of a technical book cannot hope that his writing will answer all questions on the subject involved — he must consider it sufficient if he can open a door into music itself, for it is in the music described that the real answers lie. For this very reason, some exceptional treatments of certain aspects of fugal writing in the works of the masters are first introduced in the comments upon the musical examples at the ends of chapters, for it is only in connection with the music itself that these features became meaningful. Thus, the musical examples and the comments upon them serve a dual role, first to exemplify theoretical points already made in the text, and second, sometimes to introduce new but related points, particularly of exceptional practices.

An attempt has been made in this book to leave the teacher some freedom, though care has been taken to omit no necessary information. But no matter how well and carefully a book is written and no matter how brilliant the teacher is in presenting the material involved, in the end the real mastery of any subject in music is going to depend upon the experience gained by the student through analysis of music itself and through composition. It is to be hoped that this textbook can lead the student to this inescapable fact.

The study of invention follows the study of fugue for two reasons. First, the freer invention is actually harder for most students than fugue and second, many of the Bach Inventions (particularly those in three-parts) are actually little fugues and are more easily understood after the study of fugue. In the author's classes, this reversal of the more common order of study for these two subjects has proved more effective.

# Contents

# Introduction:
## The Fugue, Preliminary Perspective

What is a fugue? How does the composer construct one? There are no easy answers to these questions since no all-inclusive definition of fugal practice is possible. The fugues of Frescobaldi, Bach, Handel, Mozart, Beethoven, Brahms, Schumann, and Hindemith (to mention but a few masters of the genre) are all quite different. Each composer is distinctive in his understanding of what a fugue might be, and the various fugues of any single composer often differ radically from each other in style and content. Yet there is a prototype of the fugue, an image which may be somewhat disembodied, it is true, but which is recognizable as the norm from which every great fugue derives. The unique features of a fugue, which give it life and meaning, are superimposed upon this prototype, but it is still recognizably present.

Just how is this "ideal" fugue constructed? First, a subject is stated unaccompanied in a single voice (it might be an instrument). Then a second voice enters with the answer, i.e., the subject transposed to the dominant key. The original voice continues with counterpoint against this answer. After this a third voice enters in turn with the subject again while both the first two voices continue with counterpoint against it. Finally, a fourth voice enters, now with the answer, while all three of the other voices accompany it with counterpoint. This ends the exposition of a "typical" fugue.

After the exposition, the composer creates a contrast by means of a brief episode. Then, to the end of the fugue, the subject enters in various voices with occasional further episodes for contrast. Finally, to end the fugue, the subject enters for its last appearance often above a pedal point.

Those who know in any detail the fugues of Bach or any other composer will recognize that this description of a fugue is a gross simplification. Yet there are many great fugues which don't differ widely from this basic plan. The questions left unanswered in this description of the prototype of the fugue are, however, so many that no student could either write or analyze a fugue successfully without a great deal of further explanation. What is the nature of the subject? What is its range, length, tonal planning, structure? How is the answer built? What are counter-subjects? How are they used? How is free counterpoint constructed? What material is used in episodes? How are episodes constructed? What is a stretto? How many voices may a fugue employ? It is to answer these and many other questions that this book has been written. The treatment of each feature of a fugue must be explored as it is handled by a variety of composers from the Baroque era to the present if something of the rich potential of the fugue is to be appreciated. Each of the following chapters is devoted to one particular aspect of fugue, and all that has been hoped for in this preliminary description and perspective is that it might serve to make possible a relating of each detail to the whole in a meaningful way.

# PART I

## *The Fugue*

# I

# The Subject

The composer designs his fugue subject in such a manner that its potential for contrapuntal development is great. When it is remembered that during the course of a fugue the subject will appear and reappear many times, it is evident that it must be free from mannerisms which might on constant repetition become irritating to the listener. Yet the subject must have a well-defined meaning, a *gestallt* or image which makes an immediate impact, even if only a few notes long.

How long may a subject be? How great a range may it have? What rhythmic designs does one find in fugue subjects? What underlying harmonic structure may fugue subjects imply? How is tonality handled? How is the form designed? Upon what notes of the scale may a subject begin? How are subjects ended or cadenced? Before one attempts to compose an original fugue or analyze an existing one, he must seriously consider these questions and attempt to arrive at meaningful answers to them. Therefore each of these questions will be considered and answered in relation to the subjects quoted at the end of this chapter.

*How long may a subject be?* Some are only four or five notes in length (see example I-1 at the end of this chapter), while others may be as much as eight or ten measures in length (see example I-4). The very short subject is going to force the composer to present it in a great many successive entries if his total form is to achieve any length. If he wants to avoid boring his listener he must either separate the successive entries of his subject with contrasting material — which might make his form fall apart — or he must achieve contrast by accompanying the appearances of his subject with designs that are sufficiently elaborate to obviate the constant repetitions.

*How great a range may a fugue subject exhibit?* A few subjects span only a fourth or fifth (see example I-1), while others may have a total range of a tenth or even more (see example I-4); but most fugue subjects stay within the range of an octave. The wider the range, the greater is the difficulty in avoiding crossing of the separate voices, a feature which tends to obscure the texture. Of course, in fugues which use sharply contrasting instruments, such voice crossings are less confusing than would be the case with fugues using more homogeneous instruments or voices.

*What rhythmic designs may a fugue subject manifest?*   Some subjects use very even note values and are smooth flowing (see examples I-1, I-3, I-4, and I-5). In these fugues, rhythmic contrast and interest are achieved in the accompanying voices as they enter. Other fugue subjects exhibit considerable rhythmic variety (see examples I-2, I-6, and I-7). Most fugue subjects avoid too much repetition of characteristic rhythmic motives, since such repetitions would, with constant restatement of the subject, become irritating.

*What underlying harmonic structure is implied in the subject?*   This is a most important question. Indeed, real skill in counterpoint follows the understanding that polyphonic textures are simultaneously horizontal *and vertical*. Bach, perhaps the greatest contrapuntalist since the Renaissance, though he uses complex and even chromatic movement of individual voices, tends to utilize a rather simple underlying chord scheme (see examples I-9 and I-11). This permits him greater freedom than would richer chord schemes. In general, the more complex the vertical structure, the more restricted is the horizontal parameter.

*How is tonality handled in the fugue subject?*   Most Baroque, Classical, and Romantic fugue subjects are basically diatonic, though they may include some chromatic non-chord tones (see examples I-1, I-3, and I-8). But some fugue subjects begin in the tonic key and clearly modulate to the dominant key (see examples I-4, I-5, and I-6). These are called *modulating subjects*. Other subjects follow the outline of the chromatic scale. Generally these follow the chromatic scale from the tonic down to the dominant, or from the dominant down to the tonic, with or without additional diatonic tones (see example I-14). These are called *chromatic subjects*. Very few dodecaphonic composers have written fugues, though there are a few (see examples I-7 and VII-18).

*How is the formal design of the subject handled?*   Some subjects are single ideas which refuse to break into parts (see examples I-1 and I-5). Others are a composite of short figures (see examples I-2, I-4, I-6, I-7, and I-8). Often one figure is the melodic inversion of another, as is the case with subject I-3, where the last four notes are the melodic inversion transposed of the first four, or in the subject shown in example III-2, where again the last four notes of the subject are the first four notes melodically inverted and stated in diminution. Frequently the various figures which make up a fugue subject are contrasted (see examples I-2, I-7, and III-6).

*Upon what note of the scale may a fugue subject begin?* While the vast majority of fugue subjects begin upon the first or fifth notes of the scale, examples can be found of subjects which begin upon any one of the seven tones of the scale.

*How are subjects ended or cadenced?* This, again, is a most important question. Most composers prefer to run the end of the subject into the following accompanying material, so that the ending of the subject is hidden, lest it detract from the subsequent entries of subject and answer. The best way to spot the ending of a subject is to find that place at which it begins to manifest, upon its subsequent entries, a different design. In a vast majority of cases, the subject ends in the initial voice before the second voice enters. In Fugue I from the *Well Tempered Clavier* of Bach, for instance (see example III-2), the second entry (in measure 2) and the third entry (in measure 4) follow the shape of the original subject as far as the beginning of the seventh beat. Therefore the subject ends upon the note E which begins the third beat of measure two. In rare cases, the subject, entering in the first voice, overlaps the answer as it enters in the second voice.

The subject may seem a brief moment in the total fugue, but it merits a great deal of attention in terms of its design, meaning, harmonic structure, tonal implications, and ending. Much of the beauty and success of the subsequent counterpoint depends upon a thorough understanding of these initial features.

The following examples show a variety of fugue subjects, some of them with their underlying harmonic implications indicated (including several chromatic fugue subjects), and a few of them in atonal idioms.

EXAMPLES FOR CHAPTER I

Example I-1: Bach, *Well Tempered Clavier*, Vol. II, No. III

Example I-2: Hindemith, *Ludus Tonalis, Fuga secunda in G*
(Reprinted by permission of Associated Music Publishers)

Example I-3: Frohberger, *Toccata in d-minor*

Example I-4: Beethoven, *String Quartet Opus 59 No. 3*

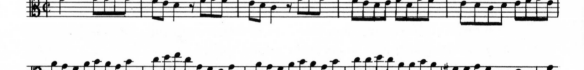

Example I-5: Mozart, *String Quartet in G-major*

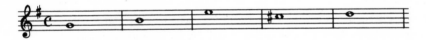

Example I-6: Bach, Cantata, *Ich hatte viel Berkümerniss*

Example I-7: Schoenberg, *String Quartet Opus 37*
(Reprinted by permission of G. Schirmer)

Example I-8: Schumann, *Fugue Opus 72 No. 1*

## Comments on Examples I-1 through I-8

I-1.  Against this brief even flow of eighth notes, Bach weaves a counterpoint of florid sixteenth and thirty-second notes.

I-2.  The subject breaks into two contrasting parts, the light staccato repeating notes and the upward motion of measure two. The repeated G's give the composer an opportunity for much oblique motion.

I-3.  Against this fast-moving but brief subject, Frohberger weaves a counterpoint of chromatically moving eighth notes mixed with slower quarter and half notes.

I-4.  An unusually long subject with a wide range. It is interesting to note that Beethoven twice reaches the note C on strong beats, the first time in measure seven as part of a tonic triad, and two measures later as part of a dominant seventh chord of the key of G-major. The subject modulates from C-major to G-major.

I-5.  A slow-moving subject which belies the fast counterpoint Mozart uses against it. This subject is also a modulating subject, moving from G-major to D-major.

I-6.  A subject with considerable rhythmic contrast. Though the note F♯ never appears in the subject, the thematic design obviously implies a modulation from C-major to G-major.

I-7.  In his *String Quartet Opus 37,* Schoenberg introduces a brief fugato, using the first six tones of set-form I³, i.e., the inversion of his original six tones transposed up three semitones.

I-8.  An effective use of rests in a subject. The G♯ in measure two does not effect a modulation, for it is immediately corrected. The subject begins and ends in D-minor.

NOTE: In the following five examples, the small notes indicate the implied harmony which in fact the composer uses.

Example I-9: Bach, *Well Tempered Clavier*, Vol. I, *No. XVII*

Example I-10: Beethoven, *Sonata Opus 110*

Example I-11: Mendelssohn, *Fugue Opus 35 No. 2*

Example I-12: Handel, *Fughetta No. 1*

Example I-13: Bach, *Well Tempered Clavier*, Vol. I, *No. XIII*

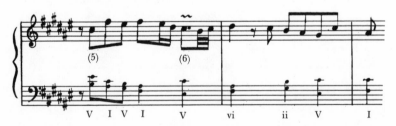

### Comments on Examples I-9 through I-13

(1) Even when this off-beat E-flat is in the bass, the chord is I, since this note is too transitory to create the impression of a second inversion triad.

(2) This E-flat, being accented and long, is harmonized with a dominant chord by Bach so that when the subject is in the bass an impossible second inversion tonic triad is avoided here.

(3) In the answer form (see next chapter), this first note is a step higher and a dominant harmony is used moving to the tonic on the second beat.

(4) Once, when the subject is in the bass, Beethoven substitutes a different chord scheme starting at this point:

$$\text{IV—ii—vii}^\circ\text{—iii—vi—V—I.}$$

But for the most part Beethoven adheres to the harmonization indicated for the various appearances of the subject.

(5) The fifth note of the scale is harmonized by a dominant harmony so that when it occurs in the bass it will not create a forbidden second-inversion tonic triad, which would be the case if both this and the following tone were harmonized as a tonic triad.

(6) Once in a later appearance this and the following tone of the subject are harmonized by the chords I–IV.

Example I-14: Chromatic subjects and their implied harmonies

NOTE: In the following example, the chromatic portions of the subjects are shown in large notes. The remainder of the subject not involved in the chromatic scale is, in each case, shown in small notes. Each subject is so aligned that the corresponding tones of the scale are directly above each other. Subjects a, b, and c involve that segment of the chromatic scale which descends from the tonic to the dominant. Subjects d and e involve that segment of the chromatic scale which descends from the dominant to the tonic. Subject f, a rare example, shows an ascending chromatic scale moving from the dominant up to the tonic.

Descending chromatically from 8 to 5 in the scale

Descending chromatically from 5 to 1 in the scale

Ascending chromatically from 1 to 5 in the scale

*Suggested Exercises for Chapter I*

1. Examine selected fugue subjects, e.g., some from Bach's *Well Tempered Clavier,* for length, range, and structure, i.e., rhythmic and melodic organization.

2. Determine the ending of the following subjects from Bach's *Well Tempered Clavier,* Vol. I:

   a. Fugue I. (Suggestion: examine the alto entry in measures 9-10.)
   b. Fugue V. (Suggestion: examine the soprano in measures 5–6.)
   c. Fugue VII. (Only examination of many entries will clarify this one!)
   d. Fugue IX. (Only at the 6th entry is the matter clarified.)
   e. Fugue XVI.

3. Write out in four-voice harmony the chord schemes given in example I-14. Let the subject be the soprano. Use such inversions of the suggested chords as will produce the smoothest effect. Write each sample a second time with the subject as the bass line.

4. Compose

   a. a short subject;
   b. a modulating subject;
   c. a chromatic subject;
   d. a subject in which a short figure in the head or beginning is featured later in its melodic inversion transposed to a new pitch;
   e. a subject featuring some rests or silence;
   f. a subject with great rhythmic contrast;

(Note: Let these be in various keys, major and minor, and various tempi, slow and fast. Mark tempi, dynamics, and phrasings in each case.)

5. Create a 12-tone set and base a subject upon it.

# II

# The Answer

When in a fugue the first voice has stated the subject a second voice enters with the answer. In its simplest form, the answer is the subject transposed up a perfect fifth or down a perfect fourth. But this is an oversimplification. Actually, there are three types of answers, each slightly different from the others: *real answers, tonal answers,* and *answers in the subdominant.* Each of these is used on quite different occasions.

The *real answer* is the exact transposition of every tone of the subject up a perfect fifth or down a perfect fourth. It is used after subjects which either avoid the fifth tone of the scale or use it only after tones 2, 4, or 6 of the scale. Examples II-1 and II-2 at the end of this chapter illustrate the real answer.

In a *tonal answer,* the fifth degree of the scale as it occurs in the subject is answered by the first degree of the scale, except when this fifth degree follows tones 2, 4, or 6, as noted in the paragraph above. The other tones of the subject have their normal answer. Tonal answers are shown in examples II-3, II-4, and II-5.

The *answer in the subdominant, i.e.,* an answer which is a perfect fourth above or a perfect fifth below the subject is used after two different types of subjects: (1) after subjects which modulate to the dominant, and (2) after subjects which begin with scale tones 5-4-5 or 5-4-3. A modulating subject has the answer in the subdominant *from the point of modulation.* The "point of modulation" may be defined as that place in the subject at which the dominant chord of the new key occurred and, in addition, as much of the subject before this dominant as served to define the approach chord to the dominant. In the subject shown in example I-5, the C♯ suggests the chord V of the key of D-major, the dominant key of the key in which the subject began, i.e., G-major. The B and E in measures 2 and 3 of the subject suggest an e-minor triad, the supertonic of D-major, the new key. In this case, then, the note B is the point of modulation and from this point on, the answer will be "in the subdominant," i.e., up a perfect fourth or down a per-

*12*

fect fifth. The answer to this entire subject reads: D-E-A-F♯-G. Example II-6 shows another modulating subject. An explanation is appended.

An *answer in the subdominant* is also customary in the case of subjects which begin with scale degrees 5-4-5 or 5-4-3. A tonal answer to these scale tones would read 1-1-2 and 1-1-7, respectively, an intolerable distortion of the shape of the subject. Example II-7 shows an answer in the subdominant of this type.

A very few fugues have answers "by inversion," "by diminution," or "by augmentation." A discussion of these unusual answers will be delayed until these special features of fugal writing are presented later in this book.

In some contemporary fugues, the answer, instead of being up a fifth (the real answer) or a fourth (answer in the subdominant), or correspondingly down a fourth or fifth, is up or down a third. This might be termed "answer at the relationship of a third." Example II-10 shows an instance of this.

A study of many fugue subjects and their answers may well confuse the beginning student, since there is a certain element of personal preference in the answers which certain composers devise. Handel, for instance, often uses a real answer where Bach would use a tonal answer. It is important to remember that the tonal answer affords an element of variety, increasing the expressive potential in the total form.

EXAMPLES FOR CHAPTER II

Example II-1: Handel, *Fughetta in C*

Example II-2: Bach, *Well Tempered Clavier,* Vol. II, *No. IX*

Example II-3: Bach, *Well Tempered Clavier,* Vol. I, *No. XXII*

Example II-4: Bach, *Well Tempered Clavier* Vol. II, *No. III*

Example II-5: Schumann, *Fugue Opus 72 No. 1*

### Comments on Examples II-1 through II-5

II-1.   A real answer. G, the fifth degree of the C-scale, is approached from D, the second degree.

II-2.   Another real answer. The fifth degree of the scale is not involved in the subject. Note that the answer begins simultaneously with the last note of the subject. The "dovetailing" of subject and answer is fairly common. In example II-1 the subject ended on the note E. Had Handel entered the answer here, the impression of a second inversion tonic triad would have been created. To prevent this illogical verticality, he marked time with the free notes C-E-F♯. These "free" notes between the end of the subject and the beginning of the answer are termed "codetta."

II-3.   A tonal answer. The fall from tonic to dominant of b-flat minor is answered by the fall from dominant to tonic of the same key, after which the answer is "real," i.e., down a perfect fourth. This affords Bach an expressive contrast between the tense rise of a minor 9th (F to G-flat) in the subject and the quieter rise of a minor 10th (B-flat to D-flat) in the answer. Note that the subject and answer are dovetailed, as was the case in example II-2.

II-4.   Usually in subjects which require tonal answers, the fifth degree of the scale occurs early in the subject, but here it is the final note. This subject outlines the complete tonic triad. When this occurs, many composers use a real answer. (See Bach, *Well Tempered Clavier*, Vol. I, *No. X*, but also *No. XVII!*)

II-5.   Another tonal answer. Schumann might well have used a real answer. The harmony in measure 5 is rather obscure in that the D-A of the soprano suggest a tonic triad, belied by the B-C of the alto.

Example II-6: Bach, *Well Tempered Clavier*, Vol. I, *No. XVIII*

Example II-7: Bach, *Organ Fugue in d-minor*

Example II-8: Bach: *Preludio con Fuga* (in E-flat)

Example II-9: Clementi, *Gradus ad Parnassum, No. 45*

Example II-10: Hindemith, *Ludus Tonalis, Fuga quarta in A*
(Reprinted by permission of Associated Music Publishers)

### Comments on Examples II-6 through II-10

II-6.  The F𝄪, while it suggests V⁷ of g♯-minor, also functions as V⁷ of iv in d♯-minor, leading in turn to iv of d♯-minor, V⁷ of d♯-minor, and finally i of d♯-minor. The modulation begins, then, on the second note of the subject.

II-7.  The typical 5-4-3 configuration (here in d-minor) which calls for an answer in the subdominant. A tonal answer here would have produced the notes D-D-D-D-D-C-D-B natural-C, an unreasonable distortion. It is interesting to note that Mozart in his *Fantasia in C major* begins a fugue subject with the notes G-F-E (tones 5-4-3). But the G is a long tone, so he gives a tonal answer, C-C-B. In similar circumstances, Handel often uses a real answer.

II-8.  From the second through the fifth notes, this subject has an answer in the subdominant. This is a rare instance in which the 3rd of the dominant triad in the subject (D in this case) is answered by the 3rd of the tonic triad (G in this case). The next few notes are adjusted to this circumstance. See Bach's *Well Tempered Clavier*, Vol. I, *No. XXIII* for a similar example.

II-9.  This subject outlines the tonic triad of c-minor and so permits a real answer. The third note of the subject, being the dominant, might be expected to have a tonal answer. But a tonal answer here would read G-B flat-C-C-C-A natural-C, which is unreasonable.

II-10.  Hindemith, in his *Ludus Tonalis* several times uses the mediant relationship for the answer.

*Suggested Exercises for Chapter II*

1. Write out selected subjects from Bach's *Well Tempered Clavier,* Vol. I (e.g., *Nos. I, II, III, IV, VII, XI, XII,* and *XIV*) , and, without reference to the answers, write out what you think the answers should be. Refer to Bach's answers and try to explain any differences between your results and Bach's.

2. Write out the answers to selected subjects from the *Well Tempered Clavier* and see if you can construct the subject which would produce such answers. This is excellent training in the relationship between subject and answer in Baroque and Classical fugues. Compare the subjects you construct from the answers with the original subjects. Do the subjects you constructed from the answers make tonal sense?

3. Write answers to the subjects you composed in response to exercise 4 in Chapter I. (Note: For the present there is no need to accompany the answer with its attendant counterpoint, which was done in all the illustrations for this chapter. The next chapter discusses the nature of this counterpoint, and after studying that, the student may attempt to continue the accompanying voice against the answer.)

# III

# The Fugal Exposition

The subject of a fugue may enter unaccompanied in any voice to begin a fugue, no matter how many voices are to be used. If the subject was stated in soprano or tenor, the answer is generally in alto or bass and vice versa. In this connection the term "voice" is used even in instrumental fugues to connote the position of the line in terms of the total texture.

While the answer is being stated, that voice which took the subject before it continues with new material. If during the course of the fugue this material which accompanies the answer is used again against subsequent statements of either subject or answer, it is called a *counter-subject;* otherwise it is called *free counterpoint.* In either case two features of its structure must constantly be kept in mind: (1) its harmonic relationship to the answer, and (2) its formal design as an independent line. In other words, it has a vertical relationship with the answer and a horizontal meaning in itself. Let us consider each of these relationships in turn.

The *vertical aspect* of the accompanying voice in relationship to the answer requires that the harmonic implications of each note of the answer be fully appreciated. The starting point is to harmonize the answer. The counterpoint against the answer, whether it is to be a counter-subject or free counterpoint, may consist of appropriate chord tones based on this harmonization interspersed with non-chord tones. It must be stressed that the very essence of good counterpoint consists in the inclusion of a high percentage of non-chord tones in the contrapuntal line, and also in the subject or answer. In this connection, consider the expressive tension created by the G♯ of the counterpoint against the F♯♯ of the answer in measure 4 of example II-6. Here the G♯ in the counterpoint is an auxiliary tone. Again, in example II-9, consider the C♯ against the G of the answer. This chromatic appoggiatura is most expressive. Remember, of course, that non-chord tones have restricted resolutions! Remember also that tones like the third and seventh of dominant seventh chords and the seventh of other seventh chords are "sensitive" tones requiring stepwise resolutions.

The *horizontal aspect* of the voice which accompanies the answer must also make sense as a thematic line. In some instances the material for this line is derived from the subject. In example II-6, when the tenor voice is finished with the subject, it continues against the answer (in the alto) by thrice stating a short figure which is derived from the 3rd, 4th, and 5th notes of the subject. In example II-1, the F♯-G in the counterpoint echoes in augmentation the half-step rise of the answer from B to C. In examples II-3, the counterpoint begins with the notes C-D flat-E flat-F, a melodic inversion of the final four notes of the subject. Likewise, in example II-8, the E flat-G-F-E flat of the counterpoint is the melodic inversion in diminution of the B flat-G-A flat-B flat of the answer. But frequently the counterpoint contrasts with the answer, being quite new material, as in examples II-2, II-7, and II-10.

The horizontal and more especially the vertical aspects of the counterpoint accompanying answers to atonal or dodecaphonic subjects will be considered in comments to examples at the end of this chapter.

When the answer and its accompanying counterpoint are completed, the composer is faced with one of three choices: (1) to state the subject again in one of the voices which have been silent up to this point; (2) to continue the exposition with another answer in one of the voices which has been resting up to this point — a relatively rare procedure; or (3) to continue for a few beats the two voices already having entered in the form of what is termed a *codetta*. Let us consider each of these choices in turn.

The third entry may be a subject stated by a voice which has been silent thus far. It may follow directly upon the completion of the answer provided the tonality at the end of the answer permits this. What is involved here? Take the case of a fugue in major mode. The original statement of the subject might begin and end on the tonic or some note of the tonic triad. Then the answer would begin and end on the dominant or some note of the dominant triad so that to begin immediately with another statement of the subject would be appropriate. That is to say, the tonic beginning of the subject would follow upon the dominant ending of the answer and a perfectly logical cadential pattern would be created. But consider the case of a fugue ending its subject with the minor tonic. The answer would end with the minor dominant tonality. For instance, a fugue in a-minor would have its answer in e-minor. The e-minor triad is not a suitable dominant for a re-entrance to a-minor. Example II-3 shows a subject in b flat-minor whose answer cadences in f-minor. An examination of the score of this fugue will reveal that Bach does not feel free to enter with the subject again immediately after the answer, but must take time for a formal modulation back to b flat-minor. In many contemporary fugues, where the vertical structures are freer, it is generally possible to let the third entry (subject) follow directly after the answer as in example III-1 and III-3.

The third entry may be an answer, though this is quite rare. In this case, the tonality at the end of the second entry (an answer) and at the beginning of the third entry (another answer) is the same, so that the connection between the two is tonally smooth. Example III-2 shows the only instance of this phenomenon in all the 48 fugues of Bach's *Well Tempered Clavier*. Example III-3 shows a somewhat similar case found in Hindemith's *Third Piano Sonata* where the second entry is an answer at the 5th above, the third entry an answer at the 9th above, and the fourth entry a subject at the original pitch, B-flat.

A *codetta* between the second and third entries is found in a vast majority of fugues. Such a codetta, consisting of a few beats of free counterpoint, serves two functions: (1) it gives the composer a chance to modulate back to the tonic key; and (2) it heightens the dramatic effect of the third entry by delaying it. How long may a codetta be? What material may be used to construct a codetta? Most codettas separating the second and third entries are from one or two beats to one or two measures in length. Bach's use of a codetta more than four measures long in the f♯-minor fugue from Volume I of the *Well Tempered Clavier* is rare indeed. Examples III-4 and III-5 show typical codettas. What is the source of the material used in these codettas? In the first example (III-4), Silcher, an early Baroque composer, uses the same figure for the codetta between the second and third entries which he had used in an earlier codetta between the first and second entries. Shifted down a fourth, this figure outlines a dominant seventh chord of g-minor, the key needed for the third entry. Mendelssohn in his *Fugue Opus 35 No. 2* for the codetta between the second and third entries uses the first six notes of the subject transposed up a fourth and stated as six eighth notes, G♯-B-E-D-C♯-B (example III-5). A study of the codettas in Bach's *Well Tempered Clavier* will reveal that most codettas are constructed from fragments of the subject or the material which accompanies the subject. Occasionally quite new material is used. It must be noted that the codetta uses only those voices which have already entered previous to its occurrence.

Against the third entry, what do the voices which made the first and second entries do? The voice which took the answer may use against the third entry the same material which was used against the answer in the previous entry. Material which is repeatedly used in a fugue to accompany appearances of the subject or answer is called a *counter-subject*. Since the head of the answer may differ slightly from the head of the subject in the case of fugues with tonal answers, the composer may either alter the head of the counter-subject to conform to the subject or answer, as the case may be, or he may choose to delay the beginning of the counter-subject until the subject or answer moves beyond its point of variation, filling in with free counterpoint until he is ready to start his counter-subject. It must be noted that if a composer uses a counter-subject at all, he generally uses it against all or most entries of the subject or answer. Let us consider what has happened thus far in the typical fugal exposition. A single voice began the exposition with the subject. Let us call this Voice I. Having completed the subject, Voice I continued with either a counter-subject or free counterpoint against the answer stated in Voice II. Then, possibly after a brief codetta in Voices I and II, the subject entered in Voice III, while Voice II went on to the counter-subject against this new entry of the subject. But, during this entry what does Voice I do? Having stated in turn the subject (as entry 1) and the counter-subject or free counterpoint (against entry 2), it may now continue with free counterpoint or with material which will be used again against subsequent appearances of subject or answer. If the latter is the case, the material is termed *counter-subject 2* while the earlier counter-subject is renamed *counter-subject 1*. In outline form the first three entries of a fugal exposition would look as follows:

*For a fugue with no counter-subjects:* (1)

| Voice I: | Subject | Free Counterpoint | Free Counterpoint |
| Voice II: | Silent | Answer | Free Counterpoint |
| Voice III: | Silent | Silent | Subject |

*For a fugue with one counter-subject:* (2)

| Voice I: | Subject | Counter-subject | Free Counterpoint |
| Voice II: | Silent | Answer | Counter-subject |
| Voice III: | Silent | Silent | Subject |

*For a fugue with two counter-subjects:* (3)

| Voice I: | Subject | Counter-subject I | Counter-subject 2 |
| Voice II: | Silent | Answer | Counter-subject 1 |
| Voice III: | Silent | Silent | Subject |

(1) Examples in Bach's *Well Tempered Clavier*, Vol. I: *Nos. I, V, XV.*
(2) Examples in Bach's *Well Tempered Clavier*, Vol. I: *Nos. XII, IX, XI, XIV.*
(3) Examples in Bach's *Well Tempered Clavier*, Vol. I: *Nos. II, XXI.*

At this point in unfolding his fugue the composer again has several choices. He may (1) consider the exposition completed if he is writing a three-voice fugue since now all voices are in and the simplest form of exposition requires merely that each voice state in turn either subject or answer; (2) even if he be writing a three-voice fugue he may allow the answer to be stated in Voice I (that which took the first entry of the subject) ; or (3) if he is writing a four-voice fugue, he is now ready for the fourth entry, an answer if the third entry was a subject, or a subject if the third entry was that rare case using an answer. Let us consider each of these choices in turn.

The exposition of the typical three-voice fugue is completed after all voices have entered once with subject or answer. At this point the composer is free to go on to his first episode, a feature of the fugue to be considered in a later chapter. But some three-voice fugues of the Baroque era extend the exposition beyond the third entry in the form of an additional statement of the answer by that voice which began the exposition with the subject. In this *extended exposition*, Voice I states the answer, Voice III (which has just completed the subject) states counter-subject 1 (if a counter-subject was used with entry two) , and Voice II states counter-subject 2 (if one was used in the previous entry) . If no counter-subjects were used, Voices II and III will use free counterpoint to accompany the answer. Example III-6 shows a three-voice fugue with two counter-subjects and an extended exposition.

In a four-voice fugue, after the first three entries are completed Voice IV enters (possibly after a brief codetta) with the answer — unless, of course, the third entry was an answer, in which case the fourth entry is a subject. If the fugue uses a counter-subject, in the fourth entry Voice III (which last stated the subject) takes it. The other two voices continue with free counterpoint, unless, of course, there was a second counter-subject, in which case Voice II takes it. Example III-7 shows a four-voice fugal exposition in which there are two counter-subjects.

In describing the material used in those voices which accompany appearances of subject or answer, we have used the term "free counterpoint." In one sense this material is "free" since it does not appear again in unaltered form; but in its source it is often far from free. Indeed, much of the "free" material is derived from the subject, the material used in codettas, or from the counter-subject if one is used. In the fugue in his *Third Piano Sonata* (example III-3) , Hindemith begins with an entry of the subject in the tenor voice. This voice continues with free counterpoint against the answer which enters in the soprano in measure 5. The material for this free counterpoint is largely derived from the two rising perfect fourths in the second measure of the subject and the last three notes of the subject. In measure 4 of the subject there begins a scale-like descent, D flat-C flat-B flat-A natural. This is taken over by the tenor voice in measure 8 as part of the free counterpoint against the answer, and again by the tenor voice in measure 11 against the third entry, an answer in the alto. This constant allusion to previously used materials is a characteristic of much of the free counterpoint in expositions. By contrast, most counter-subjects, in order to maintain their separate identity, tend to use quite new and contrasted material, as can be seen by studying example III-6.

The exposition of a fugue, then, is its opening portion in which each voice, entering in turn, has a chance to state the subject or the answer. In the extended exposition, if it is used, one and possibly more of the voices continues the exposition by further statement(s) of the subject or answer. Once the exposition is completed, the composer is free to go on with the middle portion of his fugue, and this will be described in the next chapter.

## EXAMPLES FOR CHAPTER III

Example III-1: Verrall, *Fughetta I* from *Sketches and Miniatures*
(Reprinted by permission of the New Valley Music Press)

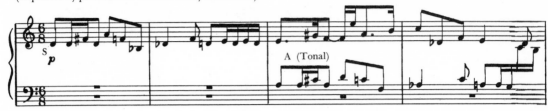

Codetta

Episode I (Lyrical)

Example III-2: Bach, *Well Tempered Clavier*, Vol. I, *Fugue I*

Example III-3: Hindemith, *Fugue* from *Piano Sonata No. 3*
(Reprinted by permission of Associated Music Publishers)

Example III-4: Silcher, *Fugue in g-minor*

Example III-5: Mendelssohn, *Fugue Opus 35 No. 2*

Example III-6: Bach, *Well Tempered Clavier*, Vol. I, *Fugue XXI*

## Comments on Examples III-5 and III-6

(1) Note the dovetailing of subject and answer. Since the final note of the subject is a note of the dominant harmony, it fits the first note of the answer (see also example III-1).

(2) Much of this material in the bass voice occurs four measures later in the tenor voice, and again three measures after that in the alto. It is, in effect, a counter-subject. However, after the exposition it does not again appear in its entirety.

(3) The beginning of counter-subject 1, when it occurs against the answer, differs from the beginning against the subject. This is because of the tonal answer. Once the third beat of subject or answer is arrived at, the difference between them ceases and the counter-subject likewise ceases to vary. In an alternative solution, Bach often delays the entry of counter-subject 1 until that portion of the answer which is tonal (and differs from the subject) is completed.

(4) Counter-subject 2 does in fact delay its entry until the tonal head of the subject is past, so that for subject or answer it can remain the same in design.

(5) In this extended exposition the voice which first took the subject (the soprano) now takes an answer. The voice which just previously to this entry took counter-subject 1 (the middle voice) now takes counter-subject 2. The bass, which last took the subject, goes on with counter-subject 1.

Example III-7: Bach, *Well Tempered Clavier*, Vol. I, *Fugue XII*

## Comments on Example III-7

(1) The downward motion, C-B natural-B flat-A-A flat-G, marks this as a chromatic subject.

(2) The first counter-subject, since it accompanies that portion of the answer which is tonal, differs when it accompanies the subject as in measure 7 in the alto voice. Only the first note of the subject is involved in a tonal answer, so from the 6th note onward, counter-subject 1 is the same for subject or answer. But note that since the answer begins in f-minor, and moves to c-minor only after its second note, the opening of counter-subject 1 involves the melodic minor scale of the f-minor tonality and only with the leap down to b-natural moves into c-minor.

(3) In the third entry, counter-subject 1 (in the alto voice) crosses below counter-subject 2. Such voice crossing is relatively rare in Bach's keyboard fugues.

(4) Only in the exposition are the first four notes of counter-subject 2 used, though they occur once again as the opening of that voice involved in free counterpoint. The remainder of the second counter-subject is sometimes split between two voices rather than being stated continuously in a single voice.

(5) At this point, an unusually long codetta begins, three measures in length.

(6) The fourth entry is a subject even though the third entry was also! This order of entries, S-A-S-S, is rare indeed. Only one other example is to be found in the "48," that is in *Fugue XIV* from Volume I.

## Suggested Exercises for Chapter III

1. In the fugues of Volume 1 of Bach's *Well Tempered Clavier,* locate all the codettas between entries one and two and describe the sources of the materials used.

2. Do the same for all codettas between entries two and three, and then for those between entries three and four.

3. Using the subject, counter-subject 1, and counter-subject 2 shown in example III-6, write out a complete entry in d-minor in which the subject is in the middle voice, the first counter-subject in the bass, and the second counter-subject in the soprano. A successful solution of this problem will require the student to study how Bach relates each subject and counter-subject to the tonality in which he couches them. It will also require a careful study of how Bach treats the melodic minor scale not only in this fugue, but in all of his fugues.

4. Repeat the problem above (no. 3) using the answer form instead of the form, i.e., start the answer on the note D.

5. Examine all the expositions in Volume I of the *Well Tempered Clavier* to see how often Bach uses
   a. extended expositions;
   b. dovetailing of subject and answer;
   c. counter-subjects.

6. Construct fugal expositions on subjects of your own, some or all of them in Baroque style.

# IV
# The Episode

In most fugues the exposition with its extension — if it has one — is followed by the first episode. Further episodes may be used later to separate the various counter-expositions in which further entries of the subject and/or answer are stated. The function of episodes is to separate further entries of the subject after the exposition, and to afford relief from that tightness of form which constant unrelieved entries of the subject would entail. It is true that some fugues have no episodes (see *Fugue I* from Volume I of Bach's *Well Tempered Clavier*), but this is rare. Most fugues have three or more episodes ranging in length from a few measures to a dozen or more measures. Many of these episodes serve the function of modulating from one key to another. Several types of design are used in episodes: free or lyrical episodes, sequential episodes, canonic episodes, episodes reappearing in double or triple counterpoint, multi-partite episodes, episodes using points of imitation, and episodes reappearing with inversion at intervals other than the fifteenth. Each of these types must be described in detail.

*Free or lyrical episodes:* These episodes unfold their designs in free counterpoint without sequence and with great variety of figurations (see example IV-1). The material might be freely derived from the subject, counter-subject, or free counterpoint which accompanies them, or it might be entirely new. Such episodes are found often in the keyboard fugues of Handel and Robert Schumann, but they are rare in the fugues of Bach.

*Sequential episodes:* This form of episode is probably the most frequently found, not only in Baroque fugues, but in fugues of later periods down to the present time. (See examples IV-2, IV-3, IV-4, IV-5, and V-1 through V-7.) The designing of sequences, a more particular and varied subject than is generally supposed, is taken up in detail in Chapter V.

*Canonic sequence* is a special case of sequence and is the form in which most canonic episodes are found (see example IV-3). In canonic episodes, *dux* (the leading voice in the canon) generally outlines the dominant triad resolving to the tonic triad. At this moment *comes* (the answering voice) enters a fifth below or a fourth above outlining the tonic triad. This tonic triad serves as the dominant of the next member of a sequence, a step below the original member. The result is a canonic sequence descending by step. Whenever the tonic is a minor triad, it changes to major mode by raising the third sometime before it is left, since the dominant triad (of the next tonic, which begins the next member of the sequence) is by definition a major chord. All of this can be seen in example IV-3 where a sequential canon between the soprano and alto voices is accompanied by a free bass voice. The technique of writing canonic sequences is discussed in greater detail in Chapter V.

Episodes in *triple counterpoint:* Many episodes involve three voices, each stating a different theme (see example IV-4). Often these three themes are repeated in later episodes in a new arrangement, that is, with the materials interchanged between voices. Considering the three themes as originally stated as "a" (the soprano voice), "b" (the alto voice), and "c" (the bass voice), a total of six interchanged versions or "permutations" of the three themes is possible:

|                 | (1) | (2) | (3) | (4) | (5) | (6) |
|-----------------|-----|-----|-----|-----|-----|-----|
| soprano voice:  | a   | a   | b   | b   | c   | c   |
| alto voice:     | b   | c   | a   | c   | a   | b   |
| bass voice:     | c   | b   | c   | a   | b   | a   |

In fugues which repeat one episode later contrapuntally inverted as triple counterpoint, generally only two or three of these permutations are used. Also, when the original three themes are inverted or "permuted," they are generally transposed to a new key at the same time. Thus, when Bach in his *Fugue XV* (see example IV-4) repeats, in episode II, the same three themes he used in episode I, he uses the key of D-major in this second permutation of the three themes. In episode IV he uses a third permutation of the same three themes, again in D-major, but now centered in a different part of the scale, as the harmonic analysis indicates. The chief problem in designing three themes to be used in triple counterpoint is to make certain that any one of the three can serve well as the bass voice. Practically, this means that whenever the fifth of a triad is used in any voice it will produce a second inversion triad when that voice is in the bass. If this is the case, care must be taken that the second inversion triad resolves correctly and has the proper stress, either as an accented cadential six-four chord or as an unstressed passing six-four chord. A more common solution of this problem is to use a high percentage of seventh chords rather than triads, for second inversion seventh chords are not so restrictive as second inversion triads.

*Multi-partite episodes* are those which break into several well-differentiated parts. Example IV-5 shows such an episode. Here Bach begins with an introductory measure showing points of imitation which never develop into true canon but lead to a second measure in which sequential material is broken off in the third measure. Then a true modulating sequence begins leading, in turn, to a brief free cadence. In *Fugue III* from the first volume of the *Well Tempered Clavier,* Bach has a fifteen-measure episode (beginning in measure 28) which breaks into three parts, each a different type of sequence.

*Points of imitation* serve as the basis for some episodes (see example IV-6). Points of imitation are tiny fragments of theme which pass from voice to voice without developing into true canons. The imitations are fragmentary and are not maintained, so that the imitations do not overlap as they do in canon. Beethoven, in the example just cited, uses such "points of imitation" in an unusually long and lovely episode in the fugue from his piano *Sonata Opus 106.* This episode serves both as a lyrical contrast to the body of the fugue preceding it and as the source of material for a counter-subject to the subject as it is unfolded in the subsequent counter-exposition.

*Contrapuntal inversion:* Sometimes an episode consisting of two themes, often accompanied by a free third voice, is so repeated in a subsequent episode that the two themes are contrapuntally inverted at the 10th, 12th, or some other interval other than the 15th (see example IV-7). To create an inversion at the 10th, one voice is moved up an octave while the other is moved down a 10th, or conversely, one voice is moved down an octave while the other is moved up a 10th. In inversion at the 12th, the second voice is moved a 12th while the first is moved an octave. The interval of inversion, always measured as a compound interval, is determined by the distance the second voice moves while the first voice moves an octave. Contrapuntal inversion necessarily changes vertical tensions and meanings, so that materials contrapuntally inverted are heard in a new context.

## EXAMPLES FOR CHAPTER IV

Example IV-1: Handel, *Fugue* from *Suite in f♯-minor*

Example IV-2: Hindemith, *Ludus Tonalis, Fuga quinta in E*
(Reprinted by permission of Associated Music Publishers)

Example IV-3: Bach, *Well Tempered Clavier*, Vol. I, *Fugue II*

### Comments on Examples IV-1, IV-2, and IV-3

IV-1.  The alto, tenor, and bass voices engage in a remarkably free episode which refuses to settle down into sequence, canon, or points of imitation, though a few of the figures used do appear twice. The material is new.

IV-2.  This is a typical "symmetrical" sequence (see Chapter V). It is the first episode following directly upon the exposition. Involved are the soprano and bass voices. The alto, which will next enter with the subject, rests. The subject begins with the notes D-B-E-A. It will be noted that these notes are used (in a new order) to begin the first member of this sequence in the soprano voice. The bass voice, like the soprano, outlines the range of a minor seventh. Note the contrast between the legato of the soprano and the staccato of the bass.

IV-3.  This is a typical accompanied modulating canonic sequence. The harmonic scheme is as follows:

```
c:V     i
   f:V     i
   B-flat:V      I
         E-flat:V      I
```

Each tonic serves in turn as the dominant of the new key. The canon is at the fifth below. The B-natural-C in the alto (in parentheses) are not a part of the canon proper. They serve to clarify the harmony. The third member of this sequence is broken off part-way through. It is in fact the beginning of the subject. Thus the sequence and the next entry of the subject are "dovetailed."

Example IV-4: Bach, *Well Tempered Clavier*, Vol. I, *Fugue XV*

Episode I

Episode II

Episode IV

Example IV-5: Bach, *Toccata in e-minor*

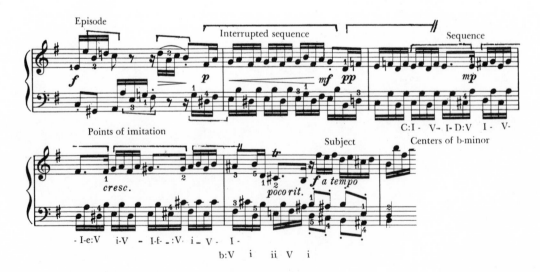

### Comments on Examples IV-4 and IV-5

IV-4.   Shown here are episodes I, II, and IV from the G-major fugue. In episode I, the bass is labeled "a" because it was derived from an earlier codetta and is a design which plays an important part throughout the fugue. Themes "b" and "c" are new material. The three permutations used in the three episodes shown are:

|           | Episode I | Episode II | Episode IV |
|-----------|-----------|------------|------------|
| Soprano:  | b         | a          | a          |
| Alto:     | c         | c          | b          |
| Bass:     | a         | b          | c          |

Each episode is in the form of a diatonic sequence of three members. But notice that the third episode shown (episode IV) is centered in the scale in a different place:

| | | | | | | | | |
|---|---|---|---|---|---|---|---|---|
| Episode I (G-major): | IV | vii$^7$ | iii | vi$^7$ | ii | V$^7$ | | |
| Episode II (D-major): | IV | vii$^7$ | iii | vi$^7$ | ii | V$^7$ | | |
| Episode IV (D-major): | | | iii | vi$^7$ | ii | V$^7$ | I | IV$^7$ |

Notice also that, in episode IV, theme "a" starts a 16-note late so that the first two notes must be stated in diminution. Theme "c" is embellished with two extra ornamental notes (shown in parentheses). In the third member of episode IV, both themes "b" and "c" are broken off. Actually, theme "a" continues for another measure beyond what is shown in this illustration before it too breaks off.

IV-5.   When the sequence finally begins in this episode (in measure 3), it starts with a C-major triad, the Neapolitan chord of b-minor. The supertonic of minor mode is always a problem in sequences, for in the harmonic minor scale it is a diminished triad. Composers often turn it into either a minor triad, or lower the root and consider it a Neapolitan chord.

Example IV-6: Beethoven, *Sonata Opus 106* (Finale)

Example IV-7: Verrall, *Fugue* from *Sketches and Miniatures*
(Reprinted by permission of the New Valley Music Press)

Episode I

Episode III (= Episode I inverted at 12th)

## *Comments on Examples IV-6 and IV-7*

IV-6.  The chief "points of imitation" are bracketed in this example, but other imitations are present. For instance, in measure 3, the soprano (E-F♯-G) states the opening of the theme given two measures earlier, but now in melodic inversion. In measure 7 the soprano echoes the last half of this same theme. Much of the material used can be traced to the theme first stated by the soprano. Only a fugue of the proportions of this one could support so long and so contrasting an episode.

IV-7.  In episode I, the "a" theme (in the soprano) is above the "b" theme (in the bass). But in episode III it is transposed down a 12th into the bass, while the "b" theme is shifted up an octave into the soprano. Episode III is the contrapuntal inversion at the 12th of episode I. Notice that the two sevenths on beats two and three of episode I become sixths in episode II. This is typical of the shifts in tension between two voices which occur in contrapuntal inversion at the 10th or 12th. A complete table of what happens to intervals when inverted at the 9th through the 15th is appended.

Orig. interval:  in inversion at the

| | 9th | 10th | 11th | 12th | 13th | 14th | 15th |
|---|---|---|---|---|---|---|---|
| 2nd inverts to prime * | | 2nd | 3rd | 4th | 5th | 6th | 7th |
| 3rd inverts to 7th | | prime | 2nd | 3rd | 4th | 5th | 6th |
| 4th inverts to 6th | | 7th | prime | 2nd | 3rd | 4th | 5th |
| 5th inverts to 5th | | 6th | 7th | prime | 2nd | 3rd | 4th |
| 6th inverts to 4th | | 5th | 6th | 7th | prime | 2nd | 3rd |
| 7th inverts to 3rd | | 4th | 5th | 6th | 7th | prime | 2nd |
| 8th inverts to 2nd | | 3rd | 4th | 5th | 6th | 7th | prime |

* Any of these intervals may appear in compound form, i.e., with the two notes separated by more than an octave.

Example IV-8: Bach, *Well Tempered Clavier*, Vol. I, *Prelude VII*

Original statement, measure 25:

Inversion at 15th, measure 56

Inversion at 13th, measure 64

Inversion at 10th, measure 35

Reinversion * at 10th, measure 39

Inversion at 11th, measure 58

Reinversion * at 13th, measure 60

* Reinversion is best defined as an inversion of the inversion at the 15th. (See comments on next page.)

## *Comments on Example IV-8*

IV-8.  Bach's *Prelude 7* from Volume I of the *Well Tempered Clavier* is in fact an introduction and a free double fugue. In it he explores many intervals of inversion and "reinversion" between the heads of the two subjects. Example IV-8 shows the various relationships Bach establishes between these two subjects. The extraneous free counterpoint has been deleted so that the two subjects alone show up more clearly. In "reinversion" what actually happens is that the interval between the two themes is changed, though they remain in the same relationship to each other as in the original. The result, as in the case of contrapuntal inversion, is a shift in tension points. To find the interval of reinversion, invert the original at the 15th and measure the reinversions against this, rather than against the original, using the table given in the comments to example IV-7. Naturally, reinversion at the 15th does not in fact exist, since such a reinversion would merely reproduce the original and be indistinguishable from it. In fugue, inversion is found chiefly in episodes and codettas in which previous fragments of themes are repeated in new contrapuntal relationships. But (as some of the following exercises will reveal), subject and counter-subject, which are normally inverted only at the fifteenth, may occasionally be presented in an inversion at the tenth or twelfth or even some other interval. Reinversion of subject and counter-subject, or of any other pair of themes, is relatively rare.

*Suggested Exercises for Chapter IV*

1. Carry out the sequence shown in example IV-2 through four complete members. (Two and a half members are shown in the example.)

2. In episode IV in example IV-4, remove the irregularities in the soprano, alto, and bass voices so that episode IV corresponds to episode II. (Note that the "c" theme uses rests instead of tying the notes over as in episode I.) Now extend episode II one full measure. Then lengthen episode IV by inserting an extra measure *before* the present beginning measure. This will make the chord scheme of episode IV correspond to that in episode II. (See comments to example IV-4.)

3. Episodes I, II, and IV shown in example IV-4 represent three of the six possible permutations of the three subjects used. Write out the three missing permutations, one in e-minor, one in b-minor, one in C-major. Study the chord schemes given in the comments to example IV-4 before beginning the new permutations. Study measure 37 in *Fugue XV* of Volume I of Bach's *Well Tempered Clavier* to see how he handles subject "a" in the minor mode. When subject "c" occurs immediately below subject "a," rests will be necessary in subject "c" as in episode II.

4. Compare the bass and alto in measure 17 of Bach's *Well Tempered Clavier, Fugue II* with the soprano and alto in measure 5. What is the interval of contrapuntal inversion used in measure 17?

5. In *Prelude VII* from Volume I of Bach's *Well Tempered Clavier*, using the alto and tenor in measure 49 as the original statement of two subjects (actually subjects II and III in a triple fugue), state what interval of inversion or reinversion is used in

  a)  measure 62, alto and bass;
  b)  measure 79, alto and bass;
  c)  measure 92, soprano and tenor. (Read the C♯ on beat 2 as D♯!)

# V

# The Sequence

The sequence plays such an important role in contrapuntal writing in general and the fugue in particular that it deserves separate treatment. The sequence, which might be defined as a design which repeats itself in some specific ascending or descending pattern, exists in the following forms:

1. Diatonic or tonal sequence
2. Modulating or real sequence
3. Symmetrical sequence
4. Partial or accompanied sequence
5. Double sequence
6. Compound sequence
7. Canonic sequence
8. Sequences with variable rates of ascent or descent
9. Sequences whose members contract vertically or horizontally.

All of these forms have certain features in common. Each consists of at least two complete *members* (statements of the basic figure or design) and the beginning of a third. Each establishes some pattern of ascent or descent which is regularly maintained. Finally, each gains its forward momentum from the fact that the ear catches the design and knows what to expect — a fact which enables the composer to introduce a surprise factor by breaking the sequence in the middle of the final member.

In *diatonic sequences* the original member repeats at some specific interval of ascent or descent, but remains throughout in one and the same key or tonality (see example V-1). The most common interval of ascent or descent is the second, i.e., a diatonic sequence ascending or descending by step. But sequences ascending or descending by thirds, fourths, or even by tritones can be found. The various voices which present the total design which constitutes the first member may not all enter at the same moment but may be slightly offset, as in example V-1. Naurally, each succeeding member repeats this feature. There is no reason that chromatic non-chord tones (i.e., chromatic auxiliary tones, chromatic cambiata or neighboring tones, etc.) cannot be introduced in diatonic sequences. Thus, a diatonic sequence ascending by step might begin with the notes C-B-C in C-major. The second member can be D-C-D or D-C♯-D, the third either E-D-E or E-D♯-E, the fourth F-E-F, and so on. In this case, the second tone of each member is conceived as the lower auxiliary tone.

In a *modulating sequence* each succeeding member after the original statement is in a new key. The problem here is to make the modulations convincing and to make the pattern of succeeding keys logical.

Two plans are commonly used to organize the chord scheme in modulating sequences. In the first, which is more frequently found, each member consists of a dominant chord (possibly preceded by an approach chord) resolving to a tonic triad, as in example V-2 where each member consists of the progression V⁷-I in the successive keys of A♭, B♭, and c. In the second plan, each member starts with the tonic triad and continues with the dominant chord of the key to be used in the succeeding member, as in example V-3, where the chord scheme is as follows:

$$\overline{\text{a: i — G: V.}^7} \quad \overline{\text{I — F: V}^7} \quad \overline{\text{I —//}}^{//}$$

1st member    2nd member    3rd member

Example V-4 shows again this second plan.

To make the succession of keys used in a modulating sequence convincing, composers choose a succession of keys whose tonics are triads in what might be termed a "master key" which controls the entire sequence. For instance, in example V-3 described above, the succession of keys is a-minor, G-major, and F-major. If the "master key" is taken to be a-minor, the tonics of these three keys are, in turn, the triads i, VII, and VI of a-minor. The "master key" might be that key used to begin the sequence, or that key used to end the sequence, as is the case in examples V-4 and V-11. One problem arises in applying the concept of a "master key" to determine the successive keys used in a modulating sequence, namely, certain triads in the master key will be diminished triads, incapable of serving as tonics. The leading-tone triads of all major keys, and of the harmonic forms of all minor keys are diminished triads. Several expedients are used to solve this problem. One is to break off the sequence just before these diminished triads are to be arrived at. A more common solution is to raise the 5th of the diminished leading tone triad of the major mode or the supertonic triad of the minor mode, and to use the leading tone triad on the lowered 7th degree of the minor mode. Occasionally, as in example V-4, the supertonic triad of the "master key" (when this is a minor mode) lowers the root a half-step to form the so-called Neapolitan chord. A typical chord scheme showing the supertonic triad of the "master key" as a minor triad is shown in the following diagram:

Chord Scheme: f: i    E♭:V⁷   I    d: V⁷    i    c: V⁷    i     //
Master Key:   c: iv         III           ii         i
             1st member     2nd member   3rd member   4th member

Occasionally, as in example V-5, one or more members of a sequence are modulatory while the others are diatonic. In the sequence in question here, the first member is in B-major. Since the tonic triad of B-major is IV in the key of F♯-major, the sequence is continued as a diatonic sequence in F♯-major.

In all the sequences above some of the triads used are major while others in corresponding positions in succeeding members are minor. Also, the rise or fall from one member to another measured in half-steps is not always the same, i.e., the rise from the first to the second member might be a half-step, the rise from the second to the third member a whole-step. But in a certain type of sequence found in contemporary music an exact distance is maintained between corresponding tones in each successive shift used to form the sequence. Such sequences might be termed *"symmetrical sequences,"* since all the members are exactly alike in structure. Example V-6 shows such a sequence in which each new member is a step and a half above its predecessor.

In *partial* or *accompanied sequences* some voices are in sequence while others are free. Example V-7 shows a partial sequence in which the bass is a seven-member diatonic sequence while the soprano and alto are free.

In a double sequence two different voices create two independent sequences which differ from each other either in the length of their respective members (see example V-8) or in the direction of their motion, one sequence ascending while the other descends (see example V-9).

In a *compound sequence* each member is made up of sub-members in sequential form (see example V-10). In the example shown each member breaks down into a sequence of four short fragments or sub-members.

*The canonic sequence* is, perhaps, the most complicated kind of sequence. It is generally found in the form of an accompanied canon, i.e., two voices are in the form of a canon while the third voice is independent of the canon. For the first episode of his *Fugue II* from the *Well Tempered Clavier,* Bach uses the soprano to set forth the leading voice of a canon *(dux,* the leader), and the alto to set forth the answering voice *(comes,* the follower). These two voices form a canon at the 5th below while the bass has a free-running accompaniment pattern. The whole is a modulating sequence in the form of an accompanied canon at the 5th below (see example IV-3). The pattern of chords forming the modulating sequence in this example is somewhat different from those hitherto encountered. Each member is a pair of keys, the dominant of the second being the tonic of the first: —

| c: V — i(I) | B♭:V —    I — | A♭: V — I |
|-------------|---------------|-----------|
| f:V —       | i(I)E♭: V     | — I       |
| 1st member  | 2nd member    | 3rd member |

A further example of a modulating sequence in the form of an accompanied canon (at the 4th above) may be seen in example V-3.

Rich as the history of the sequence has been, there are still untouched possibilities for new types. The next three examples to be discussed enter the area of the hypothetical and might be termed *sequences with variable rates of ascent or descent, sequences whose successive members contract horizontally, and sequences whose members contract vertically.* In the sequence shown in example V-12, the rate of ascent in each successive member doubles geometrically, i.e., the second member is up a half-step from the first, the third is up 1 step from the second, the fourth is up 2 steps from the third, and the fifth is up 4 steps from the fourth. In the sequence shown in example V-13, each successive member is shortened horizontally by dropping the final note of the preceding member. In the sequence shown in example V-14, the vertical span from the bottom note to the highest note in each member is contracted from a 9th to an 8th to a 7th and finally to a 6th.

It was stated earlier that a sequence has "at least two complete members . . . and the beginning of a third." Unless at least the starting point of the third member is arrived at, one cannot determine any pattern of ascent or descent for a sequence. But one does frequently find a figure or pattern which is exactly repeated higher or lower as though it were going to turn into a sequence. Such a device might be termed an *incomplete sequence* or a *quasi-sequence.*

Composers vary greatly in the extent to which they treat their fugal episodes sequentially and in the types of sequence they favor. Handel prefers the diatonic sequence if he uses sequence at all in his episodes.

Bach uses a great variety of sequences, having grasped something of the potential for variety inherent in the sequence. In the fugues of Hindemith one finds many symmetrical sequences. Haydn, Mozart, Beethoven, Schumann, and Brahms (all great contrapuntalists) are more conservative than Bach in their use of sequence. For a thorough analytical and theoretical grasp of the sequence, the student is urged to study the fugues of a variety of composers. Then he can hope to come to a fuller appreciation of the importance and expressiveness of this common contrapuntal device.

## EXAMPLES FOR CHAPTER V

Example V-1: Bach, *Well Tempered Clavier*, Vol. I, *Fugue XIII*

Example V-2: Bach, *Well Tempered Clavier*, Vol. I, *Fugue VII*

A♭: V⁷       I    B♭: V⁷       I   c: V⁷      i
(Master Key: E♭: IV                V          vi)

Example V-3: Bach, *Art of Fugue*, *Fugue IX*

a: i          G: V⁷          I        F: V⁷      I
(a: i                   VII             VI)

Example V-4: Bach, *Toccatta in e-minor*

C: I   V   I D: V   I   V   I e: V   i   V   I f♯: V   i V   I
(b:♮ II           III          iv             V)

### Comments on Examples V-1 through V-4

(1) In this example of a diatonic sequence the actual notes involved in the sequence itself are shown in large notes. The small notes are not a part of the sequence. The various voices begin their part of the sequence at different times and break off in the third member at different times. Bach's entrance into and leaving of sequences is seldom abrupt.

(2) In this modulating sequence the first member is in A-flat major, the second in B-flat major, the third in c-minor. The master key which determines the successive tonics is E-flat major, the key in use just as the sequence begins and the key to which Bach returns immediately after the passage quoted. The tonics of the three keys used in the sequence are, in terms of E-flat major, IV — V — vi, i.e., A-flat, B-flat, and c-minor.

(3) The chord scheme of this modulating sequence was described earlier in this chapter. Notice, however, that each tonic arrived at serves well as a pre-cadential chord to the following dominant chord.

(4) Notice that the alto and soprano form a canon at the 4th above, but that the alto rests after every fourth note rather than tying it over. This is an accompanied canon in the form of a modulating sequence.

(5) Since the master key in this modulating sequence is b-minor, the first member outlines the Neapolitan center.

(6) Notice how these minor triads are repeated in major form (using Picardy Thirds) so as to serve as dominants to the next key.

Example V-5: Bach, *Well Tempered Clavier*, Vol. I, *Fugue XIII*

F#:  V⁷ of IV    IV    vii⁷    iii       vi⁷    ii       V⁷    I

Example V-6: Hindemith, *Ludus Tonalis, Fuga tertia*
(Reprinted by permission of Associated Music Publishers)

Example V-7: Bach, *Well Tempered Clavier*, Vol. II, *Fugue XVII*

Example V-8: Handel, *Fugue* from *Suite in e-minor*

Example V-9: Bach, *Well Tempered Clavier*, Vol. I, *Prelude IV*

## Comments on Examples V-5 through V-9

(1) Except for the first chord, the dominant 7th of B-major (or V⁷ of IV in F♯ major), the entire sequence is in F♯-major. Many sequences, like this one, are mixed modulating and diatonic in their tonality, i.e., only certain members of the sequence modulate while the others remain in the original key.

(2) The soprano and bass are a symmetrical sequence in that, in each succeeding member, all the tones move up exactly a step and a half. Notice that the alto is not involved in the sequence. Therefore the sequence is also partial. The soprano breaks off after the second member and only the bass carries through the third member. (See the next example for a fuller description of partial sequence.)

(3) A partial sequence. Only the bass is a sequence, a diatonic sequence ascending by step. Note that the soprano and alto invert contrapuntally at the 15th half-way through the passage.

(4) The second sequence (in the bass) starts here. Each member is twice as long as those in the other sequence (in the soprano). The bass sequence descends by thirds to compensate for this.

(5) The upper sequence ascends by thirds, the lower sequence descends by thirds. This is possible harmonically because of the harmony, a diminished seventh chord which divides the octave equally. Note that in the soprano sequence the third member ends with the note D♯ instead of the expected E.

Example V-10: Bach, *Well Tempered Clavier*, Vol. I, *Fugue III*

Example V-11: Handel, *Suite in e-minor*

| b: V | i | a: V | i | G: V | I |
|------|------|------|------|------|------|
| (G major: | iii | | ii | | I) |

Example V-12: Sequence with geometric increase in rate of ascent

Example V-13: Sequence which drops one note with each repetition

Example V-14: Upward skip reduced in each successive member

### Comments on Examples V-10 through V-14

(1) Each member of the primary sequence is four beats in length. Yet each member is in itself a sequence of four members, each one beat in length. The members of the secondary sequence are shown with dotted lines. Only the soprano voice is shown, since it is the only voice involved in the compound sequence.

(2) A typical modulating sequence. But notice that it begins on a weak beat (beat 2 of a 4/4 measure) so that the second member cuts across the bar.

(3) The second member is up a half-step from the first, the next up a whole step, the next up two whole steps, the next up four whole steps, a geometric rate of ascent. Notice also that the individual members occupy only a beat and a half so that the starting points are constantly on new beats.

(4) A diatonic sequence ascending by thirds, but each succeeding member drops the final note of the previous member.

(5) A sequence ascending by minor thirds, except that each succeeding upward skip is a half-step less than its predecessor.

## Suggested Exercises for Chapter V

1. Using material from one of your own compositions or derived from any of the illustrations used in this chapter, illustrate each of the nine types of sequence listed at the beginning of this chapter.

2. Locate sequences in the *Well Tempered Clavier* and attempt to categorize and describe them accurately.

3. Convert example V-5 into a descending modulating sequence. (Suggestion: the seventh chords should be primary seventh chords. Let F♯-major be the master key so that the successive centers are B, a♯-minor, g♯-minor, and F♯-major.)

4. Convert example V-5 into an ascending modulating sequence with B-major as the master key. (Suggestion: rewrite the alto to read, in the first member, A♯-F♯, two quarter notes. Rewrite the bass to read, in the first member, C♯-F♯-B-C♯, four eighth notes.)

5. Convert example V-6 into a symmetrical sequence in which all three voices (including the alto) rise by whole steps for each succeeding member.

6. Using material of your own, create a modulating accompanied sequential canon. (Suggestion: use canon at the 5th below or 4th above. Study the key plans of examples IV-3 and V-3 to learn to control the tonality.)

7. Two common plans or chord schemes are described in Chapter V in the section on modulating sequences. Which of these two plans is the sequence in Bach's *Well Tempered Clavier,* Vol. I, *Fugue IX,* measures 13–15?

# VI

# The Counter-Exposition

Chapter III describes the fugal exposition in which the subject and answer are introduced alternately until each of the several voices has stated one or the other at least once, with or without counter-subjects. Chapter IV describes the episode, which in most fugues follows the opening exposition and which later, during the course of the fugue, separates further single or grouped statements of subject and/or answer. The present chapter deals with those portions of the fugue in which further entries of the subject and/or answer occur with or without counter-subjects. Such portions of the fugue are known as *counter-expositions*. A fugue usually has several counter-expositions separated from each other by episodes. In each of these counter-expositions, from one to several entries of the subject and/or answer occur. A number of questions which suggest themselves in regard to the counter-exposition are presented and answered in the following paragraphs.

*How many counter-expositions may one find in most fugues?* The fugue outlined in Table 1 (on page 58) has three counter-expositions separated from each other by three episodes. Many of the fugues in the *Well Tempered Clavier* have three counter-expositions. But the great organ fugues of Bach, as well as some of the fugues of the classical composers, are much longer, having several times as many counter-expositions separated by episodes.

*How many entries of subject and/or answer occur in each counter-exposition?* In Table 1, counter-exposition 1 has but a single entry while counter-exposition 2 has three entries, a subject, an answer, and another subject. The third counter-exposition has two entries, both subjects. In passing it might be mentioned that in fugues with real answers, all entries may be considered subjects except those which are paired in two keys which stand in tonic-dominant relationship to each other, such as the entries in E-major and B-major in counter-exposition 2 of Table 1. Of course, in fugues which have tonal answers, answers will be distinguished clearly in counter-expositions by their different configuration from the subject.

*57*

*What keys is one apt to find in counter-expositions?*  While Bach, in most of his fugues, prefers tonic, dominant, the relative key and its dominant, and occasionally the subdominant key, he does on occasion explore a wider range of keys, most of them fairly closely related to the original key. The Classical and Romantic composers wander a bit farther afield. Beethoven, for instance, in his fugue from *Sonata Opus 106,* which is in B-flat major, has one counter-exposition in b-minor. Where such distant digressions are made, the preceding episode may be used to effect the modulation.

*How many voices are involved in counter-expositions?*  A composer practically never reduces the texture to a single voice after the second

**Table 1**

Structure of Bach's Fugue IX, Well Tempered Clavier, Vol. I

Exposition                                   Extended Exposition

| | | | | | | | | | | |
|---|---|---|---|---|---|---|---|---|---|---|
| Sop.: | A —— Cod- | - CS —— Cod- | - - - - | S——— | CS——Cod- | - CS —— |
| Alto: | S——— CS—— etta | - - - - etta | - - - - | - A——etta | - - - - |
| Bass: | | S——— " " - - - | CS——— | - - -" -" - S——— |
| Key: | 1 E  2 B  3 E | 4 E  5 E  6 | 7 E  8 B  9 | 10 E |

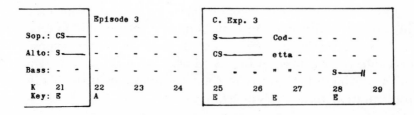

|  | Episode 1 |  | C. Exp. 1 | Episode 2 | C. Exp. 2 |
|---|---|---|---|---|---|
| Sop.: | - - - - - - - - - - | | - - - | - - - | - - - A—— |
| Alto: | - - - - - - - - - - | | S ——— | - - - | - - - - - |
| Bass: | - - - - - - - - - - | | - - - | - - - | S —— CS—— |
| Key: | 11 c#  12  13 g#  14  15 f# | | 16 c#  17 | 18 c# E | 19 E  20 B |

|  | Episode 3 | C. Exp. 3 |
|---|---|---|
| Sop.: | CS—— - - - - - - | S——— Cod- - - - - - |
| Alto: | S—— - - - - - - | CS—— etta - - - - - |
| Bass: | - ^ - - - - - - | - - - " " - - S——\|\| - |
| K 21 E | 22 A  23  24 | 25 E  26 E  27  28 E  29 |
| Key: | | |

voice enters in the original exposition, but often one or more of the voices rests during part of any given counter-exposition. This is particularly true of any voice which is later re-entered with a statement of the subject or answer. To precede such an entry with rests renders it more dramatic.

*Does one find differing formal designs in counter-expositions?* Indeed one does! Generally one finds something new in every counter-exposition, something which has not occurred up to that point. For example, in the fugue shown in Table 1, counter-exposition 1 introduces the subject for the first time in minor mode. In counter-exposition 2 the combination of answer in soprano and counter-subject in bass is new, as is the combination of counter-subject in soprano and subject in alto. In counter-exposition 3 the combination of subject in the soprano and counter-subject in the alto is new. So is the device of breaking off the final entry of the subject before its completion. This element of newness might involve finding, for subject or answer, merely a new hitherto unexplored pitch level or register. Or it might involve changes in the temporal structure of the subject such as augmentation, diminution, or the use of the device known as stating the subject *per arsen et thesin,* all of which are discussed in Chapter X. It might also involve entering a subject or answer in a new voice while it is still in progress in another voice, a device known as *stretto,* to be discussed in Chapter VIII. Also, a counter-exposition might be used to introduce a *melodic inversion* of the subject, to be described in Chapter IX, or backwards, i.e., in *retrograde motion,* a rather rare feature. Another unusual feature to be found in some counter-expositions is the ornamentation of portions of the subject or the introduction of other *anomalous statements* of subject or answer, to be discussed in Chapter VII. The final statement of the subject in the last counter exposition often occurs above a dominant or tonic pedal point and is frequently enriched by full chords, pure part writing being abandoned (see example XIII-1).

The best way to arrive at an understanding of the variety of counter-expositions to be found is to study their occurrence in many fugues. The exercises at the end of this chapter are designed to accomplish this end.

## Suggested Exercises for Chapter VI

1. In *Fugue XXI* (*Well Tempered Clavier,* Vol. I) Bach usese a subject and two counter-subjects. Though this is a three-voice fugue, the opening exposition is extended to four entries of which the 3rd and 4th set forth two permutations of the three materials, namely

|  |  |  |
|---|---|---|
| CS2 |  | A |
| CS1 | and | CS2 |
| S |  | CS1. |

After a preliminary perusal of this fugue, answer the following questions:

    a. Counter-exposition 1 (measures 22–29) explores what new permutation of these three materials? in what new key? and repeats what permutation used where earlier?

    b. Measures 22–25 are in g-minor, but both CS1 and CS2 appear in a somewhat altered form when compared with measures 9–12. Using measures 9–12 as a model, rewrite measures 22–25 to remove these changes, preserving at the same time the permutation and key used here.

    c. Compare measures 26–29 with measures 9–12. Both use the same permutation of the three materials, but in different keys. In what respect do they differ? (Hints: Consider whether subject or answer is used. Consider the tonality in both cases. Notice that when the answer form is used, the skip from the 3rd to the 4th notes is a fifth. Is that the case in measure 26? What should the 4th note have been here?) Rewrite these four measures (26–29) using measures 13–16 as a model, but preserving the permutation and beginning the answer upon the note G.

    d. Counter-exposition 2 (measures 35–45) has three entries. The first of these (measure 35–36) is peculiar in what respects? Is this a new permutation? As a practical exercise, start an answer on middle C in the alto voice, beginning in c-minor, placing CS1 in the soprano, CS2 in the bass, and complete the full four measures of this entry, using measures 13–16 as a model.

    e. What permutation is not used at all in this fugue? Write out subject, counter-subject 1, and counter-subject 2 in this missing permutation in the key of E flat-major. Then write it out again using the answer form.

2. *Fugue V* (*Well Tempered Clavier,* Vol. I) has no counter-sub-jects. How many counter-expositions are used? How many entries are used in each? What keys are used? (Hint: Consider measure 6 as a short episode, and note the unusually long episode which ends the fugue, measures 17–28.) As a practical exercise, write out on a staff the exact pitches of the first note of each entry for the entire fugue as a guide to the variety of pitch levels at which the subject occurs.

3. *Fugue VII* (*Well Tempered Clavier,* Vol. I) uses a counter-sub-ject against most statements of the subject or answer. How many coun-ter-expositions are used? How many entries of the subject or answer are used in each? (Hint: Consider measure 19 and half of 20 as a codetta so that the entries before and after are considered as a pair.) Notice in measure 20 that the counter-subject starts on the note A-flat. What note should it have started on? (See measure 6.)

4. Study selected fugues of a variety of composers, Baroque, Classical, Romantic, and Contemporary, to come to an understanding of their use of the counter-exposition.

# VII

# Anomalies in Fugal Design

One of the gravest problems in designing a fugue is the avoiding of a certain squareness of form, a predictability which risks incurring the listener's boredom. Almost from the inception of fugal writing, composers have learned to introduce certain anomalous statements into the statement of the subject, sequences, canons, and even the form it-self. The most common anomalies involve features which might be categorized as follows:

1. Changes in rhythm in the subject or answer;
2. Ornamentation of the subject or answer;
3. Simplification of the subject or answer;
4. Shifting portions of the subject or answer out of place;
5. Omitting portions of the subject or answer;
6. Repeating portions of the subject or answer;
7. Transferring the subject, answer, or counter-subject from one voice to another;
8. Introducing accidentals before certain notes of the subject or answer;
9. Introducing unusual features into the formal design of the fugue;
10. Introducing false or added tones into a canon;
11. Irregularities in a sequence.

*Changes in the rhythmic value* of the first note of a subject or answer have occurred in the works of masters from the late Renaissance to the present. Of all composers, Bach has shown the greatest imagination and variety in applying the principle of rhythmic change. Not only does he use the more common doubling or halving of the value of the first note of subject or answer, but sometimes he cuts the value of the opening note to as little as an eighth of its original value. He also alters the time value of notes other than the initial note of the subject or answer (see examples VII-1, VII-2, and VII-3).

*Ornamentation of the subject* has also existed as a common practice

62

almost from the inception of the fugue. In its commonest form it consists of filling in skips of a third with passing tones. But examples VII-3 and VII-4 show a stepwise motion later appearing ornamented by additional skips of a third.

*Simplification* of the subject consists in cutting out ornamentations, passing tones, or other fast-moving tones (see example VII-5).

*Shifting* portions of the subject is somewhat rarer. In this practice individual notes might be shifted out of position. For instance, in example VII-5 the eighth note of the subject is high C♯. But in the counter-exposition quoted it appears an octave lower (see also examples VII-6, VII-7, and VII-8).

*Omitting* portions of the subject occurs occasionally. Usually it is the middle portion of the subject which is missing (see example VII-9). An unusual and dramatic application of this principle occurs when just the head of the subject appears, often in an unexpected key, voice, or beat (see example VII-10).

*Repeating* portions of the subject is a natural extension of the previous principle, yet it is rarely found (see example VII-11).

*Transferring* the subject, answer (or even a counter-subject) from one voice to another is frequently to be found in fugues (see example VII-12).

*Introducing accidentals* before certain tones in a subject does not alter its shape, but it does affect its tonality. In example VII-14, most of the F's are changed to F♯ so that the tonality of the subject in the counter-exposition shown is not d-minor but g-minor.

*Formal anomalies* may manifest as changes in the routine order of presenting subject and answer. For instance, in the *Well Tempered Clavier*, Vol. I, the opening exposition consists of S-A-A-S instead of the more frequent S-A-S-A, while *Fugue XIII* uses the following order of entries in the opening exposition: S-A-S-S. In terms of the Classical or Baroque fugue, Hindemith's fondness for answers in the mediant in the opening exposition is anomalous. Example VII-13 shows a different formal anomaly. Many four-voice fugues present a fifth entry (usually in answer) in that voice which first presented the subject. But here one voice (the tenor) takes both subject and answer consecutively to increase the total entries to five, the final one being the answer in the bass.

Either *false or added* tones may be introduced into *comes* (the answering voice) in a canon. Bach, in *Fugue III* from the *Well Tempered Clavier*, Vol. I, shifts certain tones in *comes* a third too low in an accompanied canonic sequence (see example VII-15).

*Irregularities* may be introduced into certain members of some sequences. In example IV-4, voice "c" sometimes substitutes rests for sustained tones and in episode IV ornaments "c."

The potential of anomalous statement of materials to create variety is worthy of the composer's most serious attention.

EXAMPLES FOR CHAPTER VII

Example VII-1: Bach, *Well Tempered Clavier*, Vol. I, *Fugue IV*

Original statement of subject:

A later appearance:

(1)  Still later:

Still later:

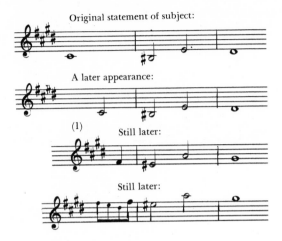

Example VII-2: Bach, *Well-Tempered Clavier*, Vol. I, *Fugue IX*

Original statement of the subject:

A later appearance:

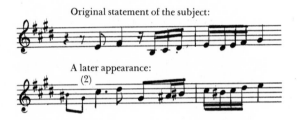

Example VII-3: Bach, *Well Tempered Clavier*, Vol. I, *Fugue XI*

Original statement:

A later appearance:

Example VII-4: Bach, *Well Tempered Clavier*, Vol. I, *Fugue VI*

Original statement of subject.

A later appearance:

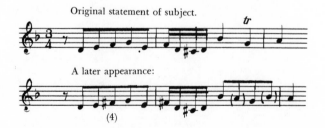

*Comments on Examples VII-1 through VII-4*

(1) Shortening or lengthening the first note of the subject in its appearances after its initial statement was common practice from the beginnings of fugal practice. But Bach carried the practice beyond this, reducing the first tone to as little as an eighth of its original value.

(2) Here, in a later appearance of the subject, the first tone is lengthened, the second tone is shortened, the rest is omitted, and the third tone is lengthened. This carries the process shown in example VI-1 far beyond its common practice.

(3) The addition of ornamental tones in this subject as it appears in a counter-exposition is rather prolific!

(4) Notice the change from F to F♯ in the first measure of this later appearance of the subject and refer to example VI-14 below. Notice also the ornamentation of the ending of the subject.

Example VII-5: Bach, *Well Tempered Clavier,* Vol. II, *Fugue XIV*

Subject as it appears in counter exposition:

(1)

As it should appear if it conformed to original statement:

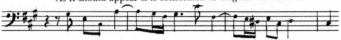

Example VII-6: Hindemith, *Ludus Tonalis, Fuga octava*
(Reprinted by permission of Associated Music Publishers)

a. Original statement of subject:

b. Later statement:

c. Still later:

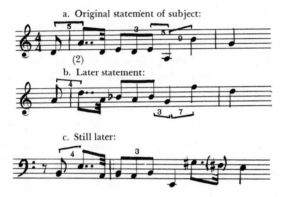

(2)

Example VII-7: Clementi, *Gradus ad Parnassum, No. 25*

Subject:

A later statement:

(3)

Example VII-8: Mendelssohn, *Fugue Opus 35 No. 2*

Original statement of subject:

A later appearance:

(4)

*Comments on Examples VII-5 through VII-8*

(1) The first line shows the subject "simplified." In measure 2 the two sixteenth notes are missing at the end of beat one. Again in measure 3 the two sixteenth notes are missing. The entire ending is simplified to cadence in f♯-minor instead of c♯-minor.

(2) The original statement of the subject rises a 5th between the first and second notes and falls a 5th between the second and third notes. At b these 5ths are contracted to 4ths, while at c the rise is a 4th, the fall a 5th. Toward the end of the subject, the rise of a 9th in the original statement later appears first as a 7th and later as a 10th.

(3) The notes B-C♯-D, the head of the subject in its original statement, appear later as A♯-B-C♯ though the rest of the subject is perfectly normal.

(4) In the statement of the subject as it appears on the lower staff, all the notes from the fourth tone onward are a step too low.

Example VII-9: Handel, *Messiah, Overture*

Original statement of subject:

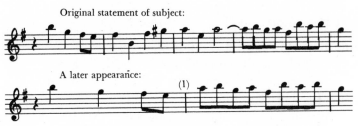

A later appearance:

(1)

Example VII-10: Bach, *Well Tempered Clavier,* Vol. I, *Fugue II*

False entry

Codetta between 2nd and 3rd entries of exposition

(2)

C.S.1

C.S.2

True entry of subject in bass

Example VII-11: Verrall, *Fugue* from *Sketches and Miniatures*

Subject:

*fz*

Answer:

added

(5)

(3)     *fz*     **(4)**

Example VII-12: Bach, *Well Tempered Clavier,* Vol I, *Fugue II*

C.S.1     (6)

C.S.2

C.S.1 continued

S

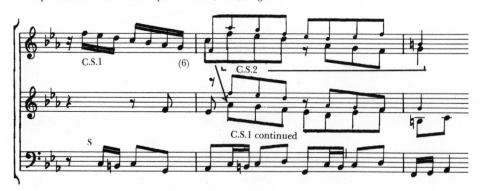

*Comments on Examples VII-9 through VII-12*

(1) Here Handel omits measures 2 and 3 of the subject, jumping directly from measure 1 to measure 4. Such a large omission is most uncommon! Where omissions do occur it is more generally in the form of that process of simplification shown in example VI-5.

(2) The head of the subject appears here in the alto voice. There are two things wrong with this: first, the subject is indeed due, but in the bass, not the alto, and second, it should occur on the last half of beat two, not beat four. So this is a "false entry."

(3) The first note is shortened from a whole note to a half note.

(4) The opening C-D flat-C-E flat are repeated before the answer goes on to the E-natural, the expected continuation.

(5) The final note should be B-flat in the answer; instead C-flat is substituted.

(6) The small notes in the soprano show counter-subject 1 as it should read if no anomalous statement were present. Actually, the notes A flat-G-F are found in the alto, which continues with counter-subject 1. Also, counter-subject 2 should appear in the alto, but actually it is transferred to the soprano. Here we see, then, a transfer of a counter-subject (counter-subject 1) from one voice to another. Such transfers may involve subject, answer, or any counter-subject.

Example VII-13: Bach, *Organ Fugue in a-minor*

Example VII-14: Schumann, *Fugue Opus 72 No. 2*

Example VII-15: Bach, *Well Tempered Clavier*, Vol. I, *Fugue III*

### *Comments on Examples VII-13 through VII-15*

(1) Four-voice fugues often have five entries — a means of simulating a five-voice fugue. But in this case the fifth entry is usually in the same voice which took the first entry. If Bach had done that in this fugue, the fourth entry (an answer) would have been in the bass (i.e., the pedals) and the fifth entry would have been in the soprano. But actually both the third and fourth entries are in the same voice, the tenor. It is most unusual to have a statement of the subject followed by a statement of the answer in one and the same voice, as it is here.

(2) The addition of accidentals to certain tones occurs on occasion. In the present case, the use of F♯ completely transforms the tonality from d-minor to g-minor. The student may examine Bach's *Well Tempered Clavier,* Vol. I, *Fugue VI,* measure 18, bass voice, for another example in which an expected C appears as C♯. In this case a tonic triad (a-minor) is transformed into the dominant seventh chord of the sub-dominant tonality, d-minor. Most accidentals transform minor triads into dominant seventh chords of a related key.

(3) In this canon certain tones are out of place, and are therefore anomalous. These include the first tone of *dux* in the soprano, which should read B♯ (shown in parentheses as a small note) and the fifth and tenth tones of *comes* in the alto, which should read F♯♯ and E♯ respectively (shown in parentheses as small notes). Bach's changes (anomalies) are for the purpose of achieving a clearer harmonic structure.

Example VII-16: Bach, *Organ Fugue in E-major*

a. Answer:

b. Counter-subject, first appearance:

c. Counter-subject, later appearance against answer:

d. Counter-subject, a still later appearance against answer:

e. Subject:

f. Counter-subject, first appearance against subject:

g. Counter-subject, an appearance in the pedals against subject:

h. Counter-subject, a later appearance against subject:

Example VII-17: Bach, *Well Tempered Clavier*, Vol. I, *Fugue I*

Original subject:

A later appearance:     (2)

Example VII-18: Verrall, *Fugue* from *Wind Septet*

### Comments on Examples VII-16 through VII-18

(1) It was stated in Chapter III that when a fugue has a tonal answer, it is necessary either to start the counter-subject after the tonal head of the answer is completed or to change the design of the beginning of the counter-subject when it appears against the answer from the form it took against the subject. But in the present example Bach goes beyond what would be necessary to make the counter-subject fit both subject and answer. The various appearances of the counter-subject show a consistent design of the beginning of the counter-subject, but a great variety in the actual pitches used.

(2) Examples VI-6, VI-7, and VI-8 showed shifts in certain portions of the subject as it appeared in counter-expositions. The present example shows a shift downward by one step *of the entire subject*. This might be termed "modal shift." Normally a subject begins on one and the same tone of the scale, no matter what key it appears in. Here the original statement of the subject begins upon the first tone of the scale, C. When the subject appears in G-major, it begins upon G. When it appears in a-minor, it begins upon A. But in the example quoted as "a later appearance" (actually measure 21), though it is in C-major, it begins upon the seventh degree of the scale.

(3) This fugue subject is based upon a 12-tone row:

C — D flat-F — E flat-D — B flat-B — E — G — F♯ — A — G♯

The subject (line 1) sets forth tones 1 through 12. In a later appearance of the subject, tones 2 through 12 plus the first tone of a transposition are used. This is very similar to the "modal shift" described above. (This is shown in line 2 of the example.)

## Suggested Exercises for Chapter VII

1. Describe the anomalies in the statement of the subject in *Fugue VI* from the *Well Tempered Clavier,* Vol. I, measures 8–10.

2. *Prelude XIX* in the *Well Tempered Clavier,* Vol. I, is an example of triple counterpoint. Consider the soprano in measure 1 as subject I, the bass starting on beat 2 as subject II, and the alto as subject III. The permutation used in measures 12–14 contains certain anomalies. Write out these measures in full score (three staves) for flute, viola, and bassoon eradicating all anomalies.

3. State the subject quoted in example VII-9 as a modal shift and add two voices in free counterpoint to make logical harmony. (See comment on example VII-17.)

4. Apply the various techniques described in this chapter to your own subjects.

# VIII
# Stretto

In a *stretto* (Italian for "to draw close") the subject or answer enters in one voice before it is completed in another voice, so that, in effect, one part of the subject is sounding against another part. Stretto, then, is a form of canon. A variety of types of stretto is to be found in some counter-expositions of many fugues. The following is a list of the most commonly found types of stretto:

1. Simple accompanied stretto
2. Grand stretto or *stretto maestrale*
3. Partial stretto
4. Stretto by melodic inversion
5. Stretto by diminution or augmentation
6. Stretto *per arsin et thesin*
7. Stretto in the opening exposition (close fugue)

A *simple accompanied stretto* begins with a statement of the subject (or answer) in any voice the composer might desire. Some several beats after this first voice begins the subject, a second voice enters with subject (or answer). Any free voice or voices may join in with free counterpoint, serving to enrich and clarify the harmony (see examples VIII-1 and VIII-2). Stretto can be described in terms of the time lag between entries and by the interval (vertically) between the first note of each entry. Thus, example VIII-1 is a stretto at the six beat lag and at the octave above while example VIII-2 is a stretto at the one beat lag and at the fourth below. The free voice(s) serve a real function in clarifying the harmony, and often their presence is essential. While the free voice may use fragments of any counter-subjects, the counter-subject in its entirety is usually dropped during counter-expositions which exhibit stretto.

In a *grand stretto* or *stretto maestrale* each voice enters in turn with the complete subject at a sufficiently close lag that for a portion of the

77

stretto all voices are sounding a portion of the subject simultaneously (see example VIII-3).

A *partial stretto* uses only a portion of the subject in stretto. Usually one voice states the subject complete while other voices enter in stretto with only the beginning of the subject (see example VIII-4). Many fugue subjects are capable of sustaining a stretto for a portion of their length. A minimum of experimentation will usually reveal some proper lag and interval of canon for a partial stretto.

*Stretto by melodic inversion* is rare, but some examples are to be found (see example VIII-5). In this type of stretto the second voice to enter states the subject inverted melodically, a device to be described in detail in Chapter IX. Briefly described, the inversion states each succeeding note of the subject in the opposite direction from its original appearance.

In *stretto by diminution* the voice to enter in stretto states the subject with all note values cut in half (see example VIII-6). In *stretto by augmentation* the note values of the voice in stretto are doubled, or, in the case of fugues in triple times, tripled (see example VIII-7).

A one beat lag will produce a stretto *per arsin et thesin* (i.e., "by accent and un-accent") in which the stressed beats of *dux* and *comes* in the canon (stretto) do not correspond. Example VIII-3 uses stretto *per arsin et thesin*.

The use of stretto is generally limited to counter-expositions. However, on rare occasions one finds the opening exposition using stretto. In this case the opening exposition is in the form of a grand stretto, and the resulting fugue is called a *close fugue* (see example VIII-8).

Many fugues do not use stretto at all, and indeed, not all subjects lend themselves to close imitation. Some fugues which use stretto limit its appearance to one of the final counter-expositions where the dramatic effect of stretto can form a proper climax to the fugue. A few fugues use stretto in all or most counter-expositions, and such fugues may be termed "stretto fugues." But in these the complexity of the stretti is carefully graduated from simple accompanied two-part stretto in earlier counter-expositions, through more complex stretti in the middle portions of the fugue, to a grand stretto in the final counter-exposition.

Most stretti are constructed as canons at the octave or at the fifth above or fourth below. But other intervals of imitation are possible provided the harmonic content can be rendered sensible. For instance, example VIII-3 shows the use of canon at the third below to form the interval at which two voices enter in stretto. The questions of what intervals of imitation are suitable and how far to carry the stretto (in the case of partial stretto) and indeed, whether to use stretto at all, must be resolved in terms of the resulting harmonic progressions. In this, experience and the willingness to experiment will bring deeper understanding of the nature and uses of stretto.

## EXAMPLES FOR CHAPTER VIII

Example VIII-1: Bach, *Well Tempered Clavier*, Vol. I, *Fugue XI*

Example VIII-2: Bach, *Well Tempered Clavier*, Vol. I, *Fugue I*

Example VIII-8: *Well-Tempered Clavier*, Vol. II, *Fugue V*

Example VIII-4: Schumann, *Fugue Opus 72 No. 4*

Original statement of subject:

### *Comments on Examples VIII-1 through VIII-4*

NOTE: In all the examples in this chapter, the subjects and answers in stretto are shown in large notes, and the voices involved in free counterpoint used as accompanying material in small notes.

(1) The soprano voice is a modified form of the counter-subject, which is, however, abandoned when the second voice enters in stretto.

(2) The stretto is at the octave above, both the bass and alto being statements of the subject. In fugues with tonal answers, stretto at the octave might involve two answers. In fugues with real answers, stretto at the octave is best considered as involving the subject, not the answer.

(3) The typical simple stretto (accompanied) at the fourth below. Stretto at the fourth below or at the fifth above involves a subject followed by the answer in stretto. The order may be reversed, i.e., a statement of the answer followed by the subject a fourth above or fifth below.

(4) Notice how the bass clarifies and enriches the harmony.

(5) A typical grand stretto. Notice that each successive entry follows rests, a fact which renders the entries clearer and more dramatic. The interval of imitation of the second and fourth entries (third below) is rather uncommon. Grand stretto usually involves imitation at the fourth below or fifth above for the second and fourth entries, making them in effect answers.

(6) The soprano voice is a complete statement of the subject, but the alto, tenor, and bass break off before completing the subject (or rather the answer). Notice the rhythmic anomalies in the soprano statement.

Example VIII-5: Bach, *Well Tempered Clavier*, Vol. I, *Fugue VI*

Example VIII-6: Bach, *The Art of Fugue, Fugue VI*

Example VIII-7: Schumann, *Fugue Opus 72 No. 1*

Example VIII-8: Handel, *Israel in Egypt*

### Comments on Examples VIII-5 through VIII-8

(1) The melodic inversion starts a fourth below the starting point of the subject in the soprano. Notice that many steps are answered by half-steps in the opposite direction and vice versa. The size of the thirds also differs. A complete description of melodic inversion will be given in Chapter IX.

(2) Notice the fragment of the subject (in a modal shift down a step) in the bass.

(3) The skip upward of a sixth in the subject is answered in the alto by a downward skip of a fifth. Such anomalies are common in stretto. The notes G-B flat-A would have been possible here if the soprano were to use F instead of F♯ and the bass were adjusted to form the chord vii$^{o7}$ of d-minor.

(4) Here the subject in the alto is followed by a stretto in diminution in the soprano.

(5) The alto enters in stretto by augmentation. This is an example of partial stretto in that neither voice involved with the subject makes a complete statement of the subject.

(6) This example quotes the complete opening exposition which is in the form of a grand stretto, making this a close fugue.

## Suggested Exercises for Chapter VIII

1. Write out the *stretto maestrale* in Bach's *Fugue XXII* from the *Well Tempered Clavier,* Vol. I, in full score. In what respect are the answers anomalous?

2. Write an accompanied simple stretto at the two beat lag at the octave below of the subject quoted in example VIII-4.

3. Start the subject shown in example VIII-5 on D in the soprano, the inversion on A at the three beat lag in the alto, using the bass voice as a free accompaniment. Write out a complete inversion stretto.

4. Using the subject of Bach's *Fugue II* from the *Well Tempered Clavier,* Vol. I, create a simple accompanied stretto at the octave below and at the one beat lag.

5. Using the subject quoted in the alto voice of example VIII-6, create an accompanied stretto by augmentation. Exploration as to the most suitable lag and interval of stretto will be necessary.

6. Explore the possibility of various types of stretto with subjects of your own composition.

7. Study and identify the type of stretto used in the following fugues from the *Well Tempered Clavier,* Vol. I:

    a. *Fugue VIII,* measures 52–55.
    b. *Fugue VI,* measures 21–24. (What is the interval of canon?)
    c. *Fugue XV,* measures 60–63.
    d. *Fugue XVI,* measures 28–29. (Notice the counter-subject.)
    e. *Fugue XX,* measures 64–70. (Notice anomalies in subject.)
    f. *Fugue XXIV,* measures 41–44.

# IX

# Melodic Inversion

Melodic inversion, i.e., the repetition of a theme in such a way that every melodic movement is taken in an opposite direction from the original, is found in some counter-expositions where subjects and answers may occur by melodic inversion; in episodes, where previously used material may be repeated in melodic inversion; in canonic passages, where *comes* may be taken by inversion; occasionally in the opening exposition of "inversion" fugues, where the answers occur by melodic inversion; and in the free counterpoint which is used to accompany other materials, where fragments may be repeated by melodic inversion.

Two basic types of melodic inversion are to be found: tonal melodic inversion and symmetrical melodic inversion. In tonal melodic inversion some of the inverted intervals may differ in half-step measure from the original intervals in that major seconds may be inverted into minor seconds and vice versa, major thirds into minor thirds and vice versa, etc. In symmetrical melodic inversion every interval in the original is duplicated exactly in the opposite direction in the inversion.

One of the basic problems in both tonal and symmetrical melodic inversions is the control of harmonic content and tonality. The common solutions to this problem differ in the case of the two types of melodic inversion. In the case of tonal melodic inversion, subjects which start on the tonic in either major or minor mode begin the melodic inversion on the dominant and vice versa (see example IX-1). The most effective starting notes for tonal melodic inversions of subjects which start on tones other than the tonic or dominant can be seen in the following table:

Scale tone of original subject:  1 2 3 4 5 6 7 8
Corresponding tones of inversion:  5 4 3 2 1 7 6 5

Thus, if in d-minor a subject begins with E-F-D-G-A (scale tones 2-3-1-4-5), the tonal melodic inversion would read G-F-A-E-D (scale tones 4-3-5-2-1, the corresponding tones from the lower line). It often happens that a composer wishes to transpose the inversion to a new key. In that case the line marked "corresponding tones of inversion" may be applied to the new key as well as to the original key. For instance, for the melodic fragment in d-minor just given, the melodic inversion in F-major would read B flat-A-C-G-F, tones 4-3-5-2-1 in the new key.

The problem of controlling the harmony and tonality in the case of symmetrical melodic inversion is resolved in a different manner. The solution in major mode and minor mode differ. In the major mode the scale tones ascending from tonic to tonic may be arranged directly above the scale tones descending from mediant to mediant, thus:

> Scale tone of original subject:  1  2  3  4  5  6  7  8
> Corresponding tones of inversion:  3  2  1  7  6  5  4  3

To ascertain the proper note for the symmetrical inversion, select the scale tones from the lower line which lie directly below the scale tones from the upper line, representing the original subject. For instance, in C-major the subject C-D-G-F-E (tones 1-2-5-4-3 from the upper line) inverts symmetrically as E-D-A-B-C (tones 3-2-6-7-1 from the lower line). Here every melodic interval is exactly inverted (see example IX-2).

There is a second solution for subjects in major mode in which only a part of the major scale is involved — the omitted portion not producing a symmetrical inversion and therefore being avoided in both subject and inversion. This second plan consists of aligning the ascending major scale from tonic to submediant for the tones of the original subject, and below, the descending scale from submediant to tonic for the tones of the symmetrical inversion, thus:

> Scale tones of original subject:  1  2  3  4  5  6
> Corresponding tones of inversion:  6  5  4  3  2  1

Example IX-3 shows a symmetrical inversion constructed by this plan. Chromatic tones can be handled easily by using either chart shown for symmetrical inversions. Tones chromatically raised in the original subject will be read as lowered for the inversion, and vice versa. Example IX-2 shows some chromatically altered tones in both the original subject and the symmetrical inversion.

The solution of the problem of symmetrical inversion in minor mode is somewhat different. Here, for the original statement, the melodic minor scale in its ascending form is lined up from dominant to dominant while the tones for finding the symmetrical inversion are aligned beneath, using the same scale (with raised 6th and 7th tones) descending from dominant to dominant thus:

Scale tones of original subject:  5  6  7  1  2  3  4  5
Corresponding tones of inversion:  5  4  3  2  1  7  6  5

Bach's use of this plan for symmetrical inversions in minor mode is shown in example IX-4.

In the case of atonal music, to invert a given subject symmetrically one may begin the inversion on any tone, taking care to make each successive note of the inversion the same interval from the preceding note as was used in the original subject between corresponding tones, but of course, taken in the opposite direction (see example IX-5).

In 12-tone music, any Inversion set form is the symmetrical inversion of any Original set form, and vice versa. Likewise, any Retrograde-Inversion set form is the symmetrical inversion of any retrograde set form, and vice versa. Example IX-6 shows the complete exposition of the fugato from Schoenberg's *String Quartet No. 4* where the answers are by inversion. The set forms are indicated and the row order numbers, along with the complete set block or set complex of all 48 set forms of the particular row used in this composition.

Often in a fugue the thematic line used in one episode will appear in a later episode in its tonal melodic inversion, sometimes in connection with quite different accompanying material (see example IX-7).

The free counterpoint in fugal expositions and episodes alike abounds with examples of short fragments which are immediately inverted, or which are inverted a short distance later. The proximity of the inversion to the original statement is an important feature here, for the material is secondary and easily forgotten (see example IX-8).

It is worth noting that many of the gigues in the suites of Bach are written in free fugal forms in which the first period sets forth the exposition and some development of the subject in direct form while the second period introduces the inversion of the subject.

The experienced composer uses a certain freedom in designing melodic inversions, introducing occasional accidentals where they might create a clearer or more expressive harmonic content, enlarging or contracting certain skips for the same reason, or discontinuing an inversion before its completion. When such anomalies are introduced into the design they must, however, be aurally convincing. The listener does not mind being deceived when the expressive effect is heightened through anomalous statement, but he does not like to be deceived arbitrarily.

## EXAMPLES FOR CHAPTER IX

Example IX-1: Bach, *Well Tempered Clavier*, Vol. I, *Fugue XV*

Measure 1, original subject:

Measure 28, tonal inversion:

Example IX-2: Clementi, *Gradus ad Parnassum, No. 73*

Example IX-3: Bach, *Invention I*

Measure 1:

Measure 3:

Example IX-4: Bach, *Well Tempered Clavier*, Vol. I, *Fugue VI*

## Comments on Examples IX-1 through IX-4

(1) The typical tonal melodic inversion of a fugue subject. The subject begins on the tonic, and the inversion begins on the dominant.

(2) A canon by inversion. *Comes* is the symmetrical melodic inversion of *dux.* The scale tones are numbered for easy reference.

(3) The 5th tone is raised a half-step in *dux,* so the corresponding 6th tone, at (4), of *comes* is lowered.

(5) The tones are numbered for comparison with the chart for this type of symmetrical melodic inversion.

(6) The subject in symmetrical inversion. The scale tones are numbered for comparison with the chart and with the original subject.

(7) These final notes should read G♯-B-A. Bach has abandoned the strict symmetrical inversion to permit a new entry in stretto in the bass.

(8) The final note, A, is missing.

(9) Notice the anomaly, A for the expected E, which would, incidentally, have been possible.

(10) A modal shift of the inverted subject. One would have expected this inverted answer to start on A, which it could have done.

Example IX-5: Hindemith, *Ludus Tonalis, Fuga decima*
(Reprinted by permission of Associated Music Publishers)

Exposition, measures 1–4

Counter exposition, measures 16–20

(1)

Example IX-6: Schoenberg, *String Quartet No. 4*
(Reprinted by permission of G. Schirmer, Inc.)

(2)

## Comments on Examples IX-5 and IX-6

(1) Two unusual features characterize this example:

    a. The inversion begins with a solo voice; usually a counter-exposition does not reduce to a single line.

    b. Not only the subject, but the entire exposition including the counter-subject is inverted.

(2) This fugato (see Chapter X) occurs toward the end of the slow movement of Schoenberg's *String Quartet No. 4*. The following table gives the 48 set forms for the row used in this work. In this fugato set forms $0^{10}$ and $I^3$ are used. Naturally, all inversion set forms are symmetrical inversions of the original set forms and vice versa. Also, all retrograde set forms are reciprocally symmetrical inversions in terms of all retrograde-inversion set forms.

```
0                                              R
0 :D C♯A B♭F E♭E  C A♭G F♯B:0
1 :E♭D B♭B F♯E  F C♯A G♯G C:1
2 :E D♯B  C G  F F♯D B♭A A♭D♭2
3 :F E C C♯A♭F♯G E♭B B♭A D:3
4 :F♯F C♯D A G A♭E C B B♭E♭4
5 :G F♯D E♭B♭A♭A F C♯C B E:5
6 :A♭G E♭E B A B♭G♭D D♭C F:6
7 :A G♯E F C B♭B G E♭D C♯F♯7
8 :B♭A F F♯C♯B C A♭E E♭D G:8
9 :B B♭F♯G D C C♯A F E E♭A♭9
10 :C B G A♭E♭D♭D B♭G♭F E A:10
11 :C♯C A♭A E D E♭B G F♯F B♭11

I                                              RI
0 :D E♭G F♯B C♯C E G♯A B♭F:0
1 :E♭E A♭G C D D♭F A B♭B F♯1
2 :E F A A♭D♭E♭D F♯B♭B C G:2
3 :F G♭B♭A D E E♭G B C D♭A♭3
4 :F♯G B B♭E♭F E G♯C C♯D A:4
5 :G A♭C B E F♯F A C D E♭B♭5
6 :A♭A C♯C F G F♯B♭D E♭E B:6
7 :A B♭D C♯F♯G♯G B E E F C:7
8 :B♭B E♭D G A A♭C E F F♯C♯8
9 :B C E E♭A♭B♭A C♯F F♯G D:9
10 :C C♯F E A B B♭D F G G♯D♯10
11 :C♯D F♯F B♭C B E♭G A♭A E:11
```

Read $0^0$ through $0^{11}$ from left to right, $R^0$ through $R^{11}$ right to left, $I^0$ through $I^{11}$ left to right, $RI^0$ through $RI^{11}$ right to left.

Example IX-7: Bach, *Well Tempered Clavier,* Vol. I, *Fugue II*

The bass in episode I:   (1)

The soprano in episode II:   (2)

(3)

Example IX-8: Mendelssohn, *Fugue in e-minor*

C.S.

(4)   f          f inv.

S

Note: This is a half-page of examples only. Comments may appear on bottom half.

### Comments on Examples IX-7 and IX-8

(1) In episode I this bass line accompanies a canonic sequence. A few measures later, in episode II, the same line, now melodically inverted and in the soprano, accompanies quite a different sequence.

(2) The melodic inversion (tonal) is shown at (2) beginning on E-flat.

(3) Notice the A-natural, an anomalous alteration of the original.

(4) The free alto voice states a figure (bracketed *f*) and then repeats it immediately as a symmetrical melodic inversion. This material does not occur again in the fugue.

### Suggested Exercises for Chapter IX

1. Write the melodic inversion (tonal) of the subjects shown in examples VII-10 (measures 4 and 5 and beat one of measure 6) and III-6.

2. Write the symmetrical inversion of the subject shown in example IX-6.

3. Write the symmetrical inversion of the subject shown in examples I-14a and I-8.

4. Write the symmetrical inversion of the subject shown in example VII-11, starting the inversion on the note C.

5. Compose a subject using one of the "0" forms of the row shown in the comments on example IX-6 and then write out the inversion.

6. Compose a subject using one of the "R" forms of this same row and then write out the inversion.

7. Compose an exposition on an original subject exploring the use of melodic inversion in the free counterpoint.

# X
# Augmentation, Diminution, Retrograde Motion

In *augmentation* and *diminution* the duration of the notes which make up a subject or melodic fragment is changed, while in melodic inversion (see Chapter IX) and *retrograde motion* the direction of the successive notes which make up a subject or melodic fragment is changed. Augmentation and diminution are temporal changes; inversion and retrograde are directional changes.

*Augmentation* may be defined as the restatement of any subject or melodic fragment with every note value doubled (see example X-1c). In subjects using eighth-note motion in compound meters such as 6/8 or 9/8, the note values in augmentation are tripled, becoming dotted quarter-notes (see example VIII-7). In a counter-exposition of Bach's *Fugue VIII* from the *Well Tempered Clavier,* Vol. I, only certain notes of the restatement of the subject are in augmentation (see example X-1b). This process might be termed *partial augmentation.* It offers the composer an intriguing new application of the process of augmentation.

*Diminution* may be defined as the restatement of any subject or melodic fragment with every note value halved (see example VIII-6). In subjects using dotted-quarter-notes in compound meters such as 6/8 and 9/8, the note values in diminution become eighth noted, cutting the note values to one-third their original value.

Either augmentation or diminution may be applied to melodic inversions or retrograde statements of the subject or any melodic fragment.

In *retrograde motion* (often called *cancrizans* or crab motion), the composer restates a given subject or fragment with the notes taken in reverse order, moving from the last note backward to the first (see example X-2). Retrograde motion is often not effective because the material stated backward sounds unnatural, and even if it does sound well, the listener doesn't recognize it in reverse so that the point is lost. Actually, the most effective use of retrograde motion is the restatement of short characteristic fragments of free counterpoint. Here, statements of the fragment in direct and retrograde motion can occur close enough to each other to be heard easily (see example X-3). The use of augmentation, diminution, and retrograde (as well as melodic inversion) with short fragments in the free counterpoint which accompanies statements of the subject or answer in fugal expositions and counter-expositions is much neglected by composers (see example X-4). That such cases are rare is not due to the lack of expressive potential inherent in the devices. It rather implies that this is an area yet to be developed in fugal writing.

# EXAMPLES FOR CHAPTER X

Example X-1: Bach, *Well Tempered Clavier*, Vol. I, *Fugue VIII*

Example X-2: Clementi, *Gradus ad Parnassum, No. 54*

Example X-3: Bach, *Well Tempered Clavier*, Vol. I, *Fugue I*

Example X-4: Beethoven, *String Quartet Opus 131*

## Comments on Examples X-1 through X-4

(1) The original fugue subject.

(2) The inversion of the answer can be recognized by the fall of a fourth instead of the fifth used in the subject. The 4th and 6th notes of this answer (marked "x") are taken by augmentation.

(3) Here an answer (note the rising fourth) is stated in augmentation.

(4) The soprano states the subject in retrograde while the bass states it in direct motion. This is in fact a stretto by retrograde motion.

(5) The figure in the soprano in large notes (marked "f") is immediately answered in the bass in retrograde motion (marked "f retro."). Both voices are engaged in free counterpoint against a statement of the subject in the tenor, the ending of which is shown.

(6) The soprano (Violin I), states a figure ("f") and immediately repeats it in diminution ("f dim."). The subject (an answer) is in the alto (Violin II).

## Suggested Exercises for Chapter X

1. Write the subject shown in example IX-la in retrograde motion from the note A. Be careful to adjust the key to this particular starting note.

2. The answer of Bach's *Fugue XVI* from the *Well Tempered Clavier,* Vol. I, is capable of stretto by diminution at the three beat lag (by altering the final note of the answer) against the subject. Write out this stretto starting the subject in the tenor in d-minor on the note A. (Hint: Regard the fourth note of the answer in diminution as a chromatic lower neighboring, i.e., auxiliary, note.)

3. The answer of Bach's *Fugue XVII* from the *Well Tempered Clavier,* Vol. I, is capable of stretto by augmentation at the one beat lag against the subject. Write out this stretto with the subject starting on the note D-flat (in the key of the subdominant) in the alto, the answer in the soprano, and a free counterpoint in the bass.

4. Write an exposition based on an original subject in which the free counterpoint explores fragments repeated in augmentation, diminution, and retrograde motion.

5. Explore the possibilities of stretto by augmentation and diminution in counter-expositions based on original subjects.

# XI

# Fugues With More Than One Subject

Fugues with two subjects (*double fugues*), three subjects (*triple fugues*), or four subjects (*quadruple fugues*) are not much different from fugues with one, two, or three counter-subjects respectively. The main difference is the way in which the additional subject or subjects are first introduced. Once they have entered, they behave exactly like counter-subjects. Two general plans are to be found for introducing the subjects in double, triple, and quadruple fugues. In the first, as many subjects as are used are introduced simultaneously as the very first entry of the fugue. In the second, every subject has its own complete exposition and often a counter-exposition or two before they are finally combined. Fugues using the first of these plans are often known as "Italian" double, triple, or quadruple fugues while fugues using the second plan are often known as "German" double, triple, or quadruple fugues.

The easiest way to come to an understanding of the *Italian double fugue* is to see the opening exposition in outline form. The following is the outline of Cherubini's *Cum Sancto Spirito* from the *Second Mass* (see example XI-1):

| | | | | |
|---|---|---|---|---|
| Sop.: | — | — | S1 | A2 |
| Alto: | — | A1 | S2 | free |
| Ten.: | S1 | A2 | free | free |
| Bass: | S2 | free | rest | A1 |

From this outline it can be seen that whatever voice states subject 1 goes on to state answer 2 while that voice which states answer 1 goes on to subject 2 and then continues with free counterpoint. The opening statement of subject 2 is followed by free counterpoint and then a period of resting to free that voice (in this case the bass) for its statement of answer 1. It is generally true of the opening exposition of the Italian double fugue that each voice states both subjects either as subject or answer. Often the opening exposition is extended to permit every voice a chance to state both the subject and answer forms of subjects 1 and 2, making a total of eight pairs of entries instead of four.

In the *German double fugue* the first subject (with or without counter-subjects) is set forth in a regular fugal exposition followed by episodes and further counter-expositions of the first subject. Then the fugue breaks off, generally with a half cadence, and the second subject is introduced in its own exposition. Following this the first and second subjects begin to combine in pairs of voices just like a subject and counter-subject and continue in combination to the end of the fugue (see example XI-2). In a variant of this form, instead of breaking the fugue off after the first subject is completely exposed, Bach often lets one voice continue as free counterpoint against the first entry of subject 2. This is the voice which first states answer 2 in the exposition of the second subject.

The *Italian triple fugue* is again easiest understood through studying an outline of the opening exposition. The following is the outline of an Italian triple fugue in Mozart's *Mass in C* (see example XI-4):

| | | | | | |
|-------|-----|------|------|------|------|
| Sop.: | S3  | rest | S1   | A2   | A3   |
| Alto: | S2  | A3   | rest | A1   | A2   |
| Ten.: | S1  | A2   | S3   | rest | A1   |
| Bass: | —   | A1   | S2   | A3   | rest |

This is an extended exposition in which the same three voices which took the three subjects at the opening come in (in the same permutation) with the answers to these respective subjects as the fifth entry. Aside from this, two points deserve mention. First, every statement of subject or answer 3 is followed by a rest in the voice which states it. Second, every voice states either in subject or answer form each of the two subjects.

The *German triple fugue* manifests a different formal plan. Here the first subject is set forth in a regular fugal exposition followed by one or two counter-expositions. Then the second subject is introduced, either with its own complete exposition followd by counter-expositions in which it is paired with the first subject, or in a counter-exposition in which it is paired with the first subject after its initial appearance. Later in the fugue the third subject is introduced, again either in a special complete exposition of its own, or as a counter-exposition in conjunction with subjects 1 and 2 after its first appearance. Bach's c♯-minor fugue from Volume I of the *Well Tempered Clavier* is a triple fugue in which subjects 2 and 3, when they are introduced, each in turn, combine immediately with subject 1 (see example XI-3). The same composer's great E-flat *Organ Fugue* (St. Anne's) introduces subjects 2 and 3 in separate expositions before combining them with subject 1. There is one peculiarity in this particular fugue: while subject 2 and subject 1 are combined after both have been introduced, and while subject 3 and subject 1 are combined after they have both been introduced, all three are never used together.

*Quadruple fugues* are so rare as to require only a passing word or two. Cherubini, in his *Credo for Double Choir* (8 voices), writes a quadruple fugue in the Italian style, all four voices being introduced simultaneously in four of the available eight voices. Alan Hovhaness in his *Prelude and Quadruple Fugue Opus 128* uses the plan in which each new subject (subjects 2, 3, and 4) is introduced in separate counter-expositions and combined there with subject 1.

It must be emphasized again that once the various subjects in a fugue with multiple subjects have been introduced, they behave exactly like counter-subjects. The composer tries to spread the various subjects among the several voices as evenly as possible, striving for constantly new permutations and points of entry. Often one of the several subjects explores stretto, and in this case the other subjects drop out temporarily.

What have been described in this chapter are the commonly found plans for introducing more than one subject into a fugue. Since every fugue is in some particular unique, it is not surprising that one will find variants upon the plans presented above. For instance, in many double fugues one pair of voices enters with subjects 1 and 2, after which the remaining two voices enter with answers 1 and 2, as can be seen in the following outline of Handel's *Fugue in g-minor* for harpsichord:

|  |  |  |  |
|---|---|---|---|
| sop.: | — | A2 | |
| alto: | S1 | free | |
| ten.: | S2 | free | Episode 1 |
| bass: | — | A1 | |

By comparing this with the outline of the double fugue in Cherubini's *Second Mass* at the beginning of this chapter, the differences will be clear. Hayden, in his *First Mass* uses the same basic plan just outlined for a double fugue, but with an extended exposition:

| sop.: | S1 | free | rest | rest | S1 |
|-------|----|------|------|------|-----|
| alto: | — | A1 | S2 | A2 | free |
| ten.: | S2 | rest | S1 | free | S2 |
| bass: | — | A2 | rest | A1 | S2 (in 10ths with tenor!) |

C. H. Graun, in an interesting double fugue quoted by Prout in his book, *Fugal Analysis,* begins with a regular exposition of two subjects in the traditional Italian style, but immediately follows this opening exposition with a further exposition of subject 1 alone, then a still further exposition of subject 2 alone, and only then a counter-exposition with the two subjects combined again.

A deep understanding of the potentials in fugues with multiple subjects can come only with analysis of many examples, comparing them carefully, and with experience gained in composing original examples.

Example XI-1: Cherubini, *Second Mass* ("Italian" double fugue)

Example XI-2: Hindemith, *Third Piano Sonata* ("German" double fugue)
(Reprinted by permission of Associated Music Publishers)

Example XI-3: Bach, *Well Tempered Clavier*, Vol. I, *Fugue IV* ("German" triple fugue)

Subject 1, measure 1

Subject 2, measure 35

Subject 3, measure 49

All three subjects combined, measure 59

Example XI-4: Mozart, *Mass in C* ("Italian" triple fugue)

### Comments on Example XI-4

(1) Notice the real answer where a tonal answer would be expected. Often fugues with multiple subjects use real answers to avoid the problem of fitting their heads together.

(2) The fifth set of entries, marking the beginning of the extension of the opening exposition.

(3) Note the anomalous ending, F-E 8th notes for the expected E.

(4) An anomalous shift to G♯ from the expected G-natural.

### Suggested Exercises for Chapter XI

1. Outline the opening exposition of an "Italian" double fugue showing your projected order of entries of the first and second subjects and answers. (Suggestion: This exercise may be done several times to show various solutions.)

2. Outline the opening exposition of an "Italian" triple fugue showing your projected order of entries of the three subjects and their answers. (Again it is suggested that several solutions be shown.)

3. *Fugue VII* from the *Well Tempered Clavier* has a counter-subject. Write out the entire exposition as it would appear if this counter-subject were the second subject of an "Italian" double fugue.

4. Write the exposition of an "Italian" triple fugue based on the three subjects shown in example XI-3. (Actually Bach writes this as a "German" triple fugue, but it could have been an "Italian" triple fugue.)

5. Write a second subject to one of your original fugue subjects and design the exposition of an "Italian" double fugue, using the two subjects.

6. In the light of the information contained in this chapter, what do you think *Prelude XIX* from Volume I of the *Well Tempered Clavier* might be?

# XII

# Glossary of Additional
# Fugal Terms and Forms

*Fughetta:* The term *fughetta* is the Italian diminutive for fugue, and therefore implies the term "little fugue." How "little" may a fughetta be? Sometimes it consists of an opening exposition (without counter-subjects), an episode, and a final group of entries. More often it has two counter-expositions separated by codettas or simple episodes (see example III-4).

*Fugato:* Often, in a basically homophonic form, a composer will introduce a brief fugal passage, usually in the form of a fugal exposition, after which he reverts to a homophonic style. Such a passage is known as *fugato*. This is especially common in the development sections of sonata forms and in certain variations in the theme and variations form. Often in a fugato the subject is treated freely with many anomalous statements. The entries are sometimes at a different tonal relationship than tonic-dominant. In one fugato, Bach has four entries, each a fourth above the previous one, beginning respectively on the notes F$\sharp$, B, E, and A.

*Accompanied Fugue:* In some fugues for chorus and orchestra, the instruments of the orchestra merely double the voices. But at other times the orchestra has independent, often quite florid material. The latter case is known as "accompanied fugue." Sometimes the accompaniment consists of free contrapuntal material, usually mobile and rhythmic in character. But at other times it is chordal and relatively static. It might be merely a bass line with a figured bass for harpsichord or organ, or the basic chordal material which lies behind the counterpoint of the fugue itself.

*Fugue on a Chorale:* There are two types of fugue based on a chorale. In the first the opening phrase of the chorale is used, often in a somewhat altered form, as the subject of the fugue. In the second type, the chorale, often stated in the pedal of the organ, is used as an accompaniment to the fugue proper, which is carried on in the other voices.

This second type is, then, a form of "accompanied fugue." The chorale on the pedals often uses four foot stops only, which has the effect of raising all the pitches an octave so that the chorale is in the middle of the texture. Frequently the several phrases of the chorale are separated by long pauses in which the fugue is developed independently. Such a fugue might also be written for orchestra and need not necessarily use a Lutheran chorale, but rather any commonly known tune, as its basis.

*Octave Fugue:* A fugue in which, in the opening exposition, the first two entries are an octave apart (and are therefore both subjects) while the third and fourth entries, at a new pitch, are also an octave apart (and are therefore both answers).

*Counterfugue (fuga contraria)* : A fugue in which the answers are taken by melodic inversion, or in which melodic inversion of the subject occurs in the opening exposition. (See Bach, *Well Tempered Clavier,* Vol. II, *Fugue III* and *The Art of Fugue,* Nos. 5, 6, and 7.) Counterfugues sometimes have the answers by inversion and augmentation simultaneously used.

*Invertible fugue (fuga inversa)* : A fugue which is capable of being stated in its entirety (including all subjects and answers with their accompanying voices, and all episodes) by melodic inversion. (See Bach, *The Art of Fugue,* Nos. 12 and 13.)

*Fuga con alcune licenze* (or *fugue libre*) : Free fugue. Beethoven uses the term to describe his fugues in *opus 106* and *133.* The term free fugue is actually relative since there is actually no "strict fugue" against which to measure any measure of "freedom." What was mentioned in the Introduction as "the prototype of the fugue" is an abstraction, a mythical textbook fugue. Nevertheless, in Beethoven's fugues (as later in those of Brahms) the subject appears many times in greatly altered form so that a certain "license" is evident when these fugues are compared with those of Bach.

*Soggetto* (or *soggietto*) : the Italian word for "subject." Haydn, in his *String Quartet Opus 20 No. 5* titles his finale *"Fuga a due Soggetti,"* i.e., fugue with two subjects — in this case an Italian double fugue.

*al rovescio:* Italian for "by melodic inversion." One sometimes finds this term placed above that counter-exposition in which melodic inversion first manifests.

# XIII
# Fugal Analysis

This is perhaps the most important part of the study of fugue, for here one passes beyond the theoretical discussion of the fugue as prototype into the scores themselves where the unique character of individual fugues is revealed. Now the significance of every technique involved in writing a fugue is seen in context. At every step in unfolding the material of a fugue, the composer is faced with alternatives, so that the potential for uniqueness is great and the discovery of a fugue's identity is the most exciting and rewarding aspect of fugal analysis.

The simplest way to approach analysis is to move from the general to the specific. The first step is to mark the beginning and ending of every appearance of subject and answer: ⌐S————⌐, ⌐A————⌐. Then locate any possible counter-subjects and mark them: ⌐CS————⌐, ⌐CS$^1$————⌐, ⌐CS$^2$————⌐. Slash marks can be used to show incomplete beginnings or endings to subjects or counter-subjects in any of their appearances: ⌐S———//, //–A————⌐, //–CS————//. Footnotes may be used to describe the exact nature of any tonal answers or variable beginnings of counter-subjects.

Next the broad formal features can be noted, the various expositions, counter-expositions, codettas, episodes, and coda being labeled in writing above the point of their beginning. The general structure of the episodes can be noted: Sequence, Modulating Sequence, Canon, Accompanied Canonic Sequence, Free, etc. Footnotes can be added to describe these features in greater detail if necessary. The episodes and counter-expositions may be numbered for later identification.

Now that the over-all details are blocked in, the student may examine the fugue for details such as anomalies in the design of any material, stretti (which may be indicated above the score where they appear), pedal points, and any special features such as augmentation, diminution, and melodic inversion, as well as any contrapuntal inversions at intervals other than the 15th. All of these features may be neatly noted at the point of their appearance, or if there is no room to do this clearly, they may be described in greater detail as footnotes.

In the case of fugues with two counter-subjects (i.e., using triple counterpoint) or with episodes using triple counterpoint, the various permutations used may be listed in a footnote with a further indication noting the permutations not used.

By this time the structure and treatment of the fugue being analyzed should be quite clear. From this point on, the analysis might be into some particular feature such as a study of the source of materials used in the free counterpoint, codettas, and episodes, or some harmonic features such as variable harmonic treatment of the subject, or a tabulation of the various pitch levels at which the subject and answer begin in their various appearances, or a study of the tonal centers used throughout the fugue. Such researches are profitable only after the basic structure of the fugue is known so that the relationship between the particular and general is evident.

One of the most important aspects of fugal analysis is the study of the organization of the tonalities used and their relationship to the total form. This is best shown not in the music itself but in the form of a diagram so that at a glance one may appreciate the total tonal plan. The plan for Bach's *Fugue IV* from *The Art of Fugue* (quoted in its entirety at the end of this chapter) might be diagrammed as follows:

Mm.  1–18  19–34  35–39  40–42  43–53  54–71  72–74  75–85  86–95
      d      F      g      d      a      F      d      a      C-d-B flat

Mm. 96–103  104–108  109–114  115–121  122–125  126–129  130–End
     g      F      d      g-F-(A)     d      g      d

Note how the B-flat in the soprano in measures 5–6 keeps the impression of d-minor alive, preventing the emergence of the expected a-minor. The brief excursion in measures 21–22 back to d-minor is transitory and the constant reference to F-major predominates. In measures 35–36 the A-flat doesn't destroy the feeling of g-minor. The E-flats in measure 56 are transitory. Measures 63–66 suggest g-minor and measure 67 a-minor, but these centers are not established. The seeming excursion into b-minor (measure 79) is really only to set up this key as the supertonic (precadential) chord for the next key center, a-minor, in measure 81. In a similar case, the A-major in measure 121 is not a key center but the dominant of the following d-minor. The modulations in this fugue are explorations of key centers contained within the original key rather than attempts to break away from that key, and this fact accounts for the tonal solidity of the entire work.

The thematic structure of this fugue is shown in the following example.

Example XIII-1: Bach, *The Art of Fugue, Fugue IV*

EPISODE IV (Accompanied sequence)

**EPISODE V** (Points of imitation)

**COUNTER EXPOSITION V** (Coda)

Tonic Pedal Point

*Bach: The Art of Fugue, Fugue IV, Comments:*

(1) The subject is the melodic inversion of the subject Bach used in *Fugue I.*

(2) The counter-subject had best be considered to start in measure 6. The material in the soprano in measure 5 appears only with answers, and then not always.

(3) This C♯ along with the B-flat of the counter-subject returns the tonality to d-minor. A comparison of the counter-subject in measure 7 with measure 13 will show that the counter-subject, whether it accompanies subject or answer, ends in the tonic.

(4) The final note of the counter-subject is not needed when it appears against the subject rather than the answer.

(5) Episode I is in two parts. The first is a canonic sequence in the form of a double canon, 4 in 2, i.e., four voices, two subjects. Part two finds the tenor and alto again as a canonic sequence, now ascending by step. It is a contrapuntal inversion at the 12th of the tenor and bass of measure 20. *Comes 1* in both these canons is by inversion.

(6) Notice that the bass here takes over as a single voice what in measures 19 and 20 was divided between two voices. Though it is now in a single voice, the canon is evident. Notice that canon 2 fits now against canon 1 at a different lag.

(7) Just a fragmentary and anomalous statement of the counter-subject.

(8) A real answer where one might have expected a tonal answer starting on F instead of G.

(9) No counter-subject here.

(10) Note the B-natural against B-flat. The key is C-major and the B-flat is a chromatic passing tone giving to the bass a momentary subdominant feeling.

(11) The counter-subject should end with a quarter-note A tied over, moving down to a quarter-note D and back to G. This ornamental ending is anomalous.

(12) The counter-subject shifts from tenor to soprano.

(13) The B-C♯ fill out the expected rise of a fourth from A to D.

(14) The alto and soprano, a canonic sequence, are the tenor and bass of measures 19–22 inverted contrapuntally at the 12th. The tenor and bass here are the same as the soprano and alto of measures 19 and 20.

(15) An anomalous shift of the ending of the subject from here to the end. All the notes are a step too high. Notice that this forces an abandonment of the counter-subject.

(16) A fragment of the counter-subject, two beats early.

(17) A real answer where a tonal answer is expected.

(18) The sudden shift to b-minor, then e-minor, and finally a-minor is dramatic. Such tonal surprises are not too common in Bach's fugues.

(19) The tenor and bass are the contrapuntal inversion at the 15th of soprano and alto.

(20) *Dux* is a third too high for these four notes, which should read D-C-B flat-A and should be, of course, in the alto.

(21) Episode IV ends here. It is an unusually long episode, 26 measures.

(22) This G♯ clarifies the tonality as a-minor, and makes this appearance of the answer a modal shift. The answer in this place should start on D, the tonic of d-minor, not F, the mediant of d-minor. The progression back to d-minor after a moment in a-minor is effected by the C♯.

(23) There is no counter-subject in this entry nor in the final entry four measures later.

## Suggested Exercises for Chapter XIII

1. The fugues in each of the following groups from the *Well Tempered Clavier,* Vol. I, are similar in plan and realization. Select at least one fugue from each group for analysis.

Group I (Triple counterpoint) : *Fugues II, III, XXI, Prelude XIX*
Group II (Special study: Episodes) : *Fugues XII, XV, XVII*
Group III (Stretto) : *Figures I, XI, XXII*

2. Make a study of several fugues from the *Well Tempered Clavier* (or any other suitable fugues) to find out whether the harmonization of the subject as represented in the vertical structure during its various appearances is the same throughout the fugue; if not, what differences occur? (Hints: (a) Omit any fugues which use triple counterpoint, since that would tend to "freeze" the harmonic implications, and (b) compare the implied harmonies of subject against answer in fugues using tonal answers.)

3. Using your experience analyzing other composers' fugues, make an outline of the formal structure for an original fugue. Include exact disposition of subjects, answers, counter-subjects (if any are desired), codettas, episodes (including exact form and structure desired), possible stretti, and any unusual features such as melodic inversion, augmentation, diminution, etc. Then compose the fugue as outlined.

# XIV

# The Fugue: Final Perspective

Can any consideration of the fugue, which has been evolving over a period of several centuries, ever be "final"? The fugue under Bach achieved a high degree of perfection and a deep expressive content, and though the memory of this has pervaded the minds of those composers since Bach, the fugue has continued to evolve. A number of composers have bent the form to their individual styles, adding to its potential in the process. To realize that the fugue is still viable, one need only remember the lyrical prowess of Brahms in combining contrapuntal expositions and development with extended homophonic episodes in the finale of his *Sonata for Violoncello,* Opus 38. These episodes, by their contrast in style and key, become the second theme in a sonata form, the first theme, development, recapitulated first theme, and coda being the fugal subject and its development. Again, the fugue which serves as the finale of Hindemith's *Third Piano Sonata* is not just another pseudo Baroque fugue but a valid statement in Hindemith's own peculiar style.

What the fugue, as a process of unfolding musical materials, may become in the future depends upon the skill, imagination, and integrity of the composers who choose to write fugues. But a number of questions may be raised to point out possible areas in which development is possible. First, in regard to the subject itself, why could it not be subjected to variation in which ornamentation, simplification, addition, deletion, and interval distortion beyond the usual anomalies might be used? The problem here would be to preserve the "identity" of the subject, for too great a variation might in fact destroy this. Or, why could not some statements of the subject or answer develop characteristic figures so that its structure would be rendered less stable and square? Examples VII-6 and VII-11 illustrate a tendency to move in this direction.

Turning next to the answer, why could not quite new points other than dominant, subdominant, or even Hindemith's favorite mediant be explored? The tension between subject and answer might be progressively enhanced from opening exposition through various counter-expositions by using less and less closely related points (i.e., pitches) at which to enter answers.

In the episodes, why could not new approaches to texture and style create new elements and degrees of variety? If the form were large enough, this might involve changes of tempo or meter or the inclusion of new materials. Beethoven made some explorations in this direction more than a century ago in some of his great "third period" fugues such as *Opus 106* and *133*. Brahms, daring fusion of homophonic and contrapuntal styles in his first *Sonata for Violoncello and Piano*, has already been mentioned as an explorer in this direction.

Medium could have a marked effect upon style and texture in the fugue. For instance, small chamber groups of unusual instruments could adapt materials to the unique capabilities of the instruments in such a manner that successive statements of certain contrapuntal features including the subject itself could be meaningfully varied. The electronic medium could utilize contrapuntal materials and devices quite beyond any players' abilities both in the areas of rhythm and texture. Or it might be possible to combine strictly designed features with aleatory materials to gain a greater formal and textural freedom.

Of course, these might be considered idle if interesting speculations. In the end it is the composer's skill and imagination alone which can lift the fugue into a new dimension of beauty and power. The fugue has played an important role in composition for a long time, and there is no reason not to believe that it will continue to do so for a long time to come.

# PART II

*Invention*

# XV
# Invention: Definition and Preliminary Description

In its most limited definition, the invention was used by Bach and by a few contemporary composers. These are contrapuntal forms in two- or three-voice texture in which the composer explores the contrapuntal potential in one or two short subjects. Notable among the works in this form are fifteen *two part inventions* and fifteen *three part inventions* (or *sinfonias*) by Bach, and a beautiful *chromatic invention* by Bartók, *Mikrokosmos* No. 145. The Bach inventions fall into three broad categories. The first might be termed additive form, being short works based on one or two subjects, divided into three or more discrete sections, each ending with a full cadence. The cadences are often designed so that, while they may be in different keys, they are all similar (see example XV-1). Inventions of the second category include those which explore canon (see example XV-2). Inventions of the third category are in effect *fughettas*, using the Italian fugue form (see Bach, *Sinfonias* Nos. III, VI, VIII, and XII). Among those in the first category, i.e., using the sectional "additive" form are some which explore double counterpoint, having two subjects (see Bach, *Inventions* Nos. *V, VI, XI, XII,* and *XV*). Among the *sinfonias* of Bach is one which has three subjects and explores these in triple counterpoint, No. *IX.* (See also Bach's *Well Tempered Clavier,* Vol. I, *Prelude XIX,* which is similar in its use of materials.)

By a broader use of the term "invention," one might consider many of the preludes of Bach to be in fact inventions, since the way of presenting and developing subjects is similar to what one finds in the *inventions* and *sinfonias*. These would include, from the *Well Tempered Clavier,* Preludes *IV, VII, IX, XI, XII, XIII, XIV, XVIII, XIX, XX,* and *XXIII* from Volume I, and *Preludes II, IV, VI, VIII, IX, X, XIX,* and *XX* from Volume II. Most of these preludes are in pure two- or three-part writing, though a few are somewhat freer in texture. All are essentially inventions in their spirit and style.

In the very broadest sense, invention is a process in which any fragment or subject or group of subjects is explored contrapuntally. Any theme, subject, or fragment might be developed by those techniques described in the next chapter, which is a detailed account of what one finds in inventions. In this sense, many sections of the development of classical sonata forms, many portions of works like Schumann's *Novelettes,* and much contemporary music such as the chamber music of Webern, Schoenberg, and others exemplify the process of invention.

Before studying in detail the techniques used in invention, it is important to come to a feeling for the style and types of invention used in this kind of composition. Examples XV-1 and XIV-2 are appended to this chapter as examples of the kind of analysis which might lead to a preliminary understanding of the process of invention. Outlines like the following will also prove helpful. It is based on Bach's *Invention III.*

*Invention III in D-major:*
Part 1, measures 1-12, cadencing in A-major.
Part 2, measures 12–24, starts in A-major, cadences in b-minor.
Part 3; measures 24–38, starts in b-minor, cadences in A-major.
Part 4, measures 38–54, starts in A-major, cadences in D-major.
(Compare measures 51–54 with measures 7–12.)
Coda: measures 54–59. (Again, the same cadence.)

Appended to this outline of the broad formal aspects of the invention under study could be some observations of a more specific nature. For this particular invention (*Invention III*) , one might note that the dominant bass pedal point in measures 5–8 is later balanced by a tonic inverted pedal point (i.e., a pedal point in the soprano) in measures 47–50; that Part 1 begins with the subject in the right hand, Part 2 with the subject in the left hand, Part 3 with the subject in the right hand, Part 4 with the subject in the left hand, and the Coda with the subject in the right hand, an alternation process maintained throughout; that the cadential patterns, measures 11–12, 23–24, 37–38, 53–54, and 58–59 are all similar.

This type of generalized analysis is an excellent prelude to the detailed, specific study undertaken in the next chapter. In this case, to move from the general to the specific will render the latter far more meaningful and clear.

## EXAMPLES FOR CHAPTER XV

Example XV-1: Bach, *Inventio I*

*Comments on Example XV-1*

(1) The subject stated in the bass in the original key.

(2) The subject shifted to the dominant and answered two beats later in the bass at the octave below.

(3) The subject in the soprano, melodically inverted.

(4) The first four notes of the subject in augmentation.

(5) Here the bass and soprano are beats 3–4 of measure 1 contrapuntally inverted at the 12th and transposed up a step.

(6) Part 2 explores a number of related keys. The general key plan, tonic-related keys-tonic, gives the total form some of the characteristics of the A-B-A form.

Example XV-2: John Verrall, *Canons* from *Sketches and Miniatures*
(Reprinted by permission of the New Valley Music Press)

### Comments on Example XV-2

(1) Definition of terms:

    a. Canon: 3 in 1 at the third below; a canon in three voices with one subject. (Measures 1–8)

    b. Canon: 4 in 1 at the fourth above; a canon in four voices with one subject. (Measures 9–14)

    c. Canon: 4 in 2 by inversion; a canon in four voices but with two subjects in which the answering voices (*comes*) imitate the leading voices (*dux*) by melodic inversion. In this case leading voices 1 and 2 (bass and tenor) are paired, as are the following voices (alto and soprano). (Measures 15–21)

    d. Canon: 2 in 1 at the fifth below; a canon in two voices with one subject.

(2) This work is one of those which can be accepted as an invention only by that extension of the definition of the term mentioned at the end of the chapter. Nevertheless, it is characterized by that "chain of canons" strung loosely together which resembles such Bach inventions as Nos. *II* and *VIII*. Inventions using canon extensively do not consist of one continuous canon, but a series of shorter canons often separated by little episodes.

### Suggested Exercises for Chapter XV

1. Indicate the main formal features of Bach's *Invention VII*, showing how it divides into parts and indicating the tonalities used. (Hints: The formal cadence which ends Part 1 is easy to find. Using this cadence as a model, locate the cadence which ends Part 2. Compare this with the final cadence. Also note the use of pedal point in this invention.)

2. *Invention II* by Bach uses canon. Mark the beginning of *dux*, the leading voice, and of *comes*, the following voice. Then mark the ending of these, showing exactly where the soprano becomes a free voice, unanswered. The second canon begins in the bass, but is anomalous in regard to its first note, which should be a third higher than it is. Mark the beginnings and endings of *dux* and *comes* in this canon, and indicate what parts of both bass and soprano are free. Canon 3 begins like canon 1 in the soprano and uses the same material. Mark the beginning and end of *dux* and *comes* for this canon, and show where each voice becomes free to form the short coda. (The form is roughly the ABA form.)

3. Bach's *Invention IX* explores double counterpoint, the soprano in measures 1–4 being subject 1, the bass subject 2. Indicate the various appearances of these two subjects throughout the form. Compare measures 17–20 with 9–12 and note carefully the similarities and differences. Compare measures 23–24 with 21–22, again noting similarities and differences.

4. Bach's *Sinfonia III* is a free fughetta. Mark all the entries of the subject. There is a counter-subject. Mark all its appearances.

5. Bach's *Invention V* is a fughetta (Italian style ) in two voices. Subject 1 is in the soprano, subject 2 in the bass. Compare measure 5 with measure 1, and rewrite the bass in measure 1 so that the missing notes are replaced. (Hint: Replace the two E-flats with the proper running passage in 16th notes.) Measures 9–11 constitute episode 1. How does measure 9 relate to measure 5? Rewrite measure 8 so that it corresponds in design with measure 4, i.e., correct the anomalies in the bass part in measure 8 and adjust the soprano to fit the new version, using measure 4 as a model. Compare the last six measures with measures 1 to 4.

# XVI

# The Process of Invention

*(An Outline of the Techniques Involved)*

I. Given a subject for an invention, one may state it in one voice and
then further unfold it by:

A. *Restatement* in another voice, accompanied by free counterpoint,

   1. In the original key but in a different register. (See example
   XV-1, and also Bach, *Inventions III, IV, VII,* and *XIII* at
   the moment the second voice enters with the subject.)

   2. In a new key, usually the dominant. (See Bach, *Invention X.*)

   3. In the original key or in a new key, but shifted within the
   scale in the form of a *modal shift,* i.e., a subject which might
   normally begin on the tonic, for instance, might be shifted
   up a third so that it would begin on the mediant. (In example XV-1, compare the soprano of measure 8, beats 3
   and 4 with the opening statement of the subject in measure 1. In measure 1 the subject begins on the tonic of C-
   major; in measure 8 the subject begins on the supertonic of
   G-major.)

B. *Extension* of the subject itself:

   1. By repeating or continuing a melodic figure in the subject,
   usually

      a. At the end of the subject. (See example XV-1, measure 4,
      bass voice where the four note head of the subject, in
      augmentation, is extended to six notes; or measure 6
      where the soprano extends the melodic inversion of the
      final few notes of the subject, continuing it two extra
      beats.)

      b. At the beginning of the subject, where the number of
      notes involved in the anacrucis can be increased. (See
      Bach, *Invention III,* measures 12–13, bass voice, where

the expected anacrucis A-B leading to C♯ on the following strong beat is extended to read E-F♯-G♯-A-B.)

2. By lengthening the note value of the first note in the subject. (See Bach, *Invention IX,* measure 12, beat 3, soprano, where the first note of the subject instead of being a 16th note in length is a quarter-note tied to a sixteenth.) (Note: Theoretically, notes other than the first could be lengthened, though care would have to be taken not to destroy the identity of the subject.)

3. By treating a figure on the subject sequentially. (See example XV-1, measures 19–20, soprano, where the entire subject is treated as a sequence; also *Invention III,* measures 19–21, soprano, where the second measure of the subject is omitted and the first measure continued sequentially.) (Note: Review Chapter V, "The Sequence.")

C. *Melodic inversion* of all or a part of the subject. (See example XV-1, measure 9, soprano, beats 1 and 2 and compare with the statement in measure 1.)

1. Sometimes the inverted subject or fragment is stated against free counterpoint in the other voice or voices, as was the case in the example just noted, from example XV-1.

2. Sometimes, in the case of inventions with two subjects used in double counterpoint, only one of them is inverted while the other is stated in its original form. (See Bach, *Invention XI,* measure 4 with anacrucis, soprano, which is a statement of subject 2 melodically inverted, as can be seen by comparing it with the bass in measures 1 and 2. The bass in measures 3 and 4 is a statement of subject 1.) (Note: Review Chapter IX, "Melodic Inversion.")

D. *Augmentation and Diminution* (see Chapter X).

1. Theoretically the entire subject might be subjected to augmentation or diminution, though in none of the Bach inventions is this the case.

2. A portion of the subject, usually the ending, may be subjected to augmentation or diminution in what is termed partial augmentation or partial diminution. (In Bach's *Invention XV,* measures 3–4 and the first two beats of measure 5, bass voice, the subject, first given in the soprano two measures earlier, is restated in the dominant key with the last five notes in augmentation.)

3. Short fragments derived from the subject may appear later

in augmentation or diminution. (See example XV-1, measure 3, bass, in which the head of the original subject is stated in augmentation.)

E. *Retrograde* or *retrograde inversion* (see Chapter X).

1. The entire subject might be stated in retrograde or retrograde inversion, though in none of the Bach inventions or sinfonias is this done.

2. Short fragments are sometimes found which are the retrograde or retrograde inversions of earlier statements. (See Bach, *Invention XV,* measure 4, beat 1, soprano, a figure which is the retrograde of measure 2, beat 4.)

F. *Ornamentation* (i.e., the elaboration or embellishment of the subject or portions of the subject).

1. Auxiliary tones or other embellishments can be added to slow-moving notes in a subject. (In Bach's *Invention XV,* which explores two subjects in double counterpoint, subject 2 is first stated in the bass beginning with four slow notes, B-D-E-D. In measure 3 the soprano takes subject 2 now richly ornamented. Still, the outline of the original subject is plainly audible, now in the dominant key, F♯-A-B-A.)

2. Two successive notes a third or fourth apart may be filled in by passing notes.

G. *Simplification:* The reverse of F above is theoretically possible and is a device available for the composer's use. For instance, in Bach's *Invention XV* just cited, the bass in measures 1 and 2 might well have appeared first in its more ornamental form (as seen in measures 3 and 4) and later in its simplified form. Such a device, to be effective, would have to involve a subject which in its ornamental form had focal points so well defined that when they were heard alone in simplified form they would be heard as the same material.

H. *Interval distortion,* i.e., altering the size of characteristic leaps in a subject.

1. The subject as a whole may be restated with certain characteristic leaps increased or decreased in size. (In Bach's *Invention IX* the soprano first states subject 1, which contains two upward leaps of a sixth. Later, in measure 9, the first of these leaps appears as a 10th, the second as a downward skip of a third.)

2. A small fragment of a subject containing a characteristic

leap may be extracted from a subject and repeated several times in succession with the size of the leap changed with each repetition. (See Bach, *Invention XI*, measures 8 and 9, soprano, in which a fragment from the ending of subject 2 — which first appeared in the bass — is repeated three times, first with the original upward leap of a 4th, then an upward leap of a 6th, and finally an upward leap of an octave.)

I. *Extraction*, i.e., selecting some characteristic figure from the subject for separated development and restatement. These might be

  1. Subjected to any of the devices mentioned in the outline above, IA through IH.

  2. Developed as sequences. (Review Chapter V.)

J. *Canon*, in which the subject begins in one voice as *dux*, the leading voice of a canon, and at a few beats lag enters in canon form in the second voice as *comes*, the following voice.

  1. The interval of imitation is generally the octave above or below (as in Bach's *Inventions II, VIII,* and *XIV*), though any interval of imitation is available to the composer.

  2. The canon is generally broken after a few measures and taken up again after a short episode of free counterpoint. When it commences again, it is generally with the original subject, but often in another voice and another key. The result is a series of short canons separated by brief episodes.

  3. The easiest way to design such canons is to write first that portion of *dux* which stands alone before *comes* enters. Then transfer this to the other voice as the beginning of *comes*. After this the continuation of *dux* may be composed against the opening of *comes*. Again, this continuation may then be transferred to *comes*. And thus, bit by bit, *dux* is composed and immediately transferred to *comes*.

II. An invention may be built out of two subjects, first stated together in two voices and developed as *double counterpoint* or *invertible counterpoint*. When the subject originally stated in the bass is later stated in the soprano, and the subject originally stated in the soprano is later stated in the bass, i.e., when the two are contrapuntally inverted, they may be

A. Inverted at the 15th and in the original key, which is to say, each voice has been shifted an octave so that they have reversed their relationship to each other. (See Bach, *Invention*

*V,* in which subject 1, first in the bass in measures 1–4, is repeated in the soprano, measures 5–8, while subject 2, first in
the soprano in measures 1–4, is repeated in the bass, measures
5–8, the whole passage being in E-major.)

B. Inverted at the 15th but transposed to a new key. (See Bach,
*Invention VI,* measures 21–24, which is the inversion at the
15th transposed up a fifth to the dominant.) This fact can be
checked by comparing the intervals between the voices in measure 1, an octave, a major 6th, and a diminished 5th, with the
intervals between the two voices in measure 21, a unison, a
minor 3rd, and a diminished 4th. The vertical intervals formed
by the conjunction of two subjects become, when the two subjects are inverted at the 15th, also inverted as follows:

1. The unison inverts into the octave, and vice versa,
2. A second inverts into a seventh,
3. A third inverts into a sixth,
4. A fourth inverts into a fifth,
5. A fifth inverts into a fourth,
6. A sixth inverts into a third,
7. A seventh inverts into a second.

C. Inverted at the 12th, i.e., contrapuntally inverted in such a way
that one of the subjects moves down an octave into the other
voice, while the other subject moves up a 12th. The inversion
at the 12th may then appear transposed into another key. (See
example XV-1, measure 8, beats 3 and 4, which are the inversion at the 12th of measure 1, beats 3 and 4, but transposed
to a new pitch.) When two subjects are inverted at the 12th,
the vertical intervals formed by the conjunction of the two
subjects become inverted as follows:

1. The unison or octave inverts into a fifth or twelfth,
2. The second inverts into a fourth,
3. The third inverts into a third,
4. The fourth inverts into a second,
5. The fifth inverts into an octave,
6. The sixth inverts into a seventh,
7. The seventh inverts into a sixth.

D. Inverted at the 10th, i.e., contrapuntally inverted in such a way
that one of the subjects moves down an octave into the other
voice, while the other subject moves up a 10th. The inversion
at the 10th may then be transposed. When two subjects are in-

verted at the 10th, the vertical intervals formed by the conjunction of the two subjects become inverted as follows:

1. The unison or octave inverts into a tenth or third,
2. The second inverts into a second,
3. The third inverts into an octave,
4. The fourth inverts into a seventh,
5. The fifth inverts into a sixth,
6. The sixth inverts into a fifth,
7. The seventh inverts into a fourth.

E. Inverted at some interval other than the 15th, 12th, or 10th, which are, however, the commonest intervals of inversion. Tables showing how each interval inverts at any interval of contrapuntal inversion can easily be worked out by allowing one note of any given interval to remain fixed while the other is moved above it by the distance represented by the interval of inversion.

F. Reinverted. A pair of subjects may be inverted at the 15th and later *reinverted* to their original relative position by some interval *other than a 15th*. The result leaves the two subjects in their original relative position but separated by a different distance than at first.

III. Three subjects may be used in an invention, stated together at first in three voices and then restated in various permutations of the three subjects, either in the original key, or transposed to new keys. A total of six permutations of three subjects are possible, though all six seldom appear in any one composition. The six permutations of three subjects are as follow:

<pre>
Soprano:  1  1  2  2  3  3
   Alto:  2  3  1  3  1  2
  Tenor:  3  2  3  1  2  1
</pre>

(See Bach, *Sinfonia IX,* and *Prelude XIX* from the *Well Tempered Clavier,* Vol. I, which is in reality an invention or sinfonia using triple counterpoint.)

IV. In an invention all or some of the techniques described above may be applied to the subject or to any fragment of the subject. The form is built almost exclusively out of the subject or material derived from it, though brief episodes of free material may be used either to form cadences at any section of the form or as an episode between two sections. The basic spirit of the invention is the maximum exploitation of limited materials.

*Suggested Research Problems and Exercises for Chapter XVI*

1. Each of the following passages from the *Fifteen Inventions* of Bach illustrates the techniques described in this chapter. Study the passages listed and describe in details the technique or techniques used:

   a. *Invention I,* measures 15–18. (Two basic techniques are involved.)

   b. *Invention I,* compare measures 11–12 with 3–4; then describe the technique used in measures 11–12 in terms of measures 3–4.

   c. *Invention I,* measure 19: compare it with measure 3 and also describe the source of the material in terms of the original subject of this invention.

   d. *Invention XII,* measure 9: write out this measure as it would be if it exactly restated measure 1 in the key of f♯-minor and then describe what actually does happen.

   e. *Invention XII,* measure 14, beats 3 and 4: compare with beats 1 and 2 of the first measure. (See section II-F in Chapter XVI.)

   f. *Invention IX,* measures 12–14. (Compare with measures 1–3 and study Chapter XVI, section I-H.)

   g. *Invention VIII,* measures 1–11: what irregularities occur in *comes?* What is the interval of canon at the beginning? at the end of the passage? Where does *dux* break off and become free to form the cadence?

   h. In the same invention, mark the beginning and endings of both *dux* and *comes* in any further canons used.

   i. *Invention VII:* the size of the skip from the 6th to the 7th notes (a fifth, E-B) is often altered in later appearances. How many distortions of this interval can you find?

2. Invert measures 3–4 of *Invention I* at the 12th.

3. Invert measures 18–22 of *Invention IV* at the 10th, starting the subject (see measure 1) upon the note E, using F-major as the tonality.

4. Invert measures 5–10 of *Invention IV* at the 15th and then reinvert them at the 12th. In the reinversion use F-major for the first two measures, g-minor for the next two, and F-major after that to the end.

5. In *Invention VII,* measure 13, beats 3 and 4, Bach starts what might have become a modulating sequence, each member of which is two beats long. Using beats 3 and 4 as the first member of a modulating sequence, continue the passage for four members, using e-minor as the "master" or controlling tonality. (Review Chapter V, particularly the

section on modulating sequences.) (Suggestion: Reverse the order of the first two soprano notes making them D-B instead of B-D to correct this anomaly, and in member three, starting in the soprano B-G, consider this as the Neapolitan chord in f♯-minor.)

6. In *Sinfonia IX* by Bach, in measures 3 and 4 the first statement of the three subjects occurs, subject 1 in the soprano, subject 2 in the alto starting on the second quarter of the measure, and subject 3 in the bass starting on the second half of beat two. One of the six possible permutations of these three subjects is not used in this example of triple counterpoint. Write out the missing permutations in A-flat major, also in b-flat-minor.

7. Using the soprano of measure 1 of *Sinfonia VI* of Bach as a subject, compose the opening of an invention illustrating sections IA1 and IA2 from Chapter XVI.

8. Using the same subject illustrate the following sections of the outline in Chapter XVI:

    a. IA3
    b. IB1a
    c. IB1b
    d. IC1 (a tonal melodic inversion)
    e. IC1 (a symmetrical melodic inversion)
    f. IE1, retrograde (use the subject transposed up a fifth for this problem)
    g. IH1 (there is only one interval to distort).

9. Using the same subject as problem 7 uses, compose an entire invention using Bach's *Invention I* or *Invention III* as a model. Then compare your finished invention with Bach's *Sinfonia VI* and you will see some of the significant differences between Bach's treatment of subjects in the inventions and the sinfonias.

10. Using the right-hand part of Bach's *Sinfonia I* as subject 1 and the left-hand part as subject 2 (one measure only), compose an invention exploring double counterpoint, using Bach's *Invention V* as a model.

11. Using the first three measures of the soprano of Bach's *Sinfonia XIII* as *dux*, compose a canonic invention; using *Inventions II* or *VIII* as a model.

12. Consider the soprano of *Invention XI* of Bach as subject 1 (measures 1 and 2), the bass as subject 2. Then compose a third subject to stand between them as subject 3, using longer note values. Using these three subjects, compose a sinfonia using Bach's *Sinfonia IX* as a model.

13. Using the second violin part of example IX-6 through beat 1 of measure 2 as the subject of a two-part invention, and the rest of measures 2 and 3 as the continuation, complete a two-part invention in the 12-tone idiom, making constant reference to the row-blocs shown in the comments on this example. (Note: Whenever any of the set-forms — there are 48 shown — is begun, use the tones in the order given, but do not feel obliged to complete it, since incomplete rows are often found in 12-tone writing. It would be wise to indicate each set-form used and number the tones. An invention in 12-tone idiom should not be beyond the student at this stage of experience.)

14. For further experience, the student may now compose two- and three-part inventions either in Baroque style or using more contemporary techniques.

15. The student should analyze in detail as many of the Bach inventions and sinfonias as possible — a difficult task to complete, since one is always finding new details in these remarkable compositions!

# APPENDIX

# Suggested Supplementary Readings

COCKSHOOT, JOHN V. *The Fugue in Beethoven's Piano Music,* Routledge and Kegan Paul, London, 1959. A description of all the fugues, fughettas, and fugatos in Beethoven's piano music, along with ample illustrations, makes this a useful study of that master's fugal techniques: Especially interesting is a chapter entitled "Fughettas, Fugatos, Canons, and Short Passages of Imitative Writing," which serves as an excellent supplement to Chapter XII of this book.

ERICKSON, ROBERT. *The Structure of Music: a Listeners Guide,* The Noonday Press, New York, 1955. Excellent supplemental readings in the meanings of contrapuntal terms and processes with illuminating illustrations and descriptions. Especially helpful are the remarks on rhythmic structure in counterpoint. Illustrations from the Renaissance through the first half of the twentieth century.

GRAVES, JR., WILLIAM L. *Twentieth Century Fugue, A Handbook,* The Catholic University of America Press, Washington, D.C., 1962. This book is especially rich in illuminating examples from recent music with comments on newer contrapuntal techniques.

HIGGS, JAMES. *Fugue,* The H. W. Gray Company, New York. Three chapters are of especial use because of their ample illustrations and many insights: those entitled "Episode," "Stretto," and "Construction of the Fugue as a Whole."

KENNAN, KENT. *Counterpoint,* Prentice-Hall, Englewood Cliffs, New Jersey, 1959. This book would be especially useful in conjunction with the study of invention and canon. Chapters of interest in this connection are entitled "The Single Melodic Line," "Exercises in Two-Part Counterpoint," "Motive Development," "The Two-Part Invention," and "The Three-Part Invention." A useful chapter on canon describes canons in two voices, three voices, accompanied canon, and canons using special devices.

KITSON, C. H. *Invertible Counterpoint and Canon,* Oxford University Press, London, New York, and Toronto, 1928, 1947. This would serve as a good review and orientation in contrapuntal inversion and canon, though it is limited to inversion at the 15th, 10th, and 12th. The chapter on triple-counterpoint points up some of the problems which arise in the harmonic content when contrapuntal inversions are used. A chapter on imitation (i.e., free imitation) is of special interest in connection with the study of invention, as is the very practical chapter on canon.

KRENEK, ERNST. *Studies in Counterpoint,* G. Schirmer, Inc., New York, 1940. A most useful study of invention in the 12-tone idiom with chapters on the basic principles of constructing tone-rows, designing melodies and combining them in serial technique using contrapuntal forms in two-part and three-part textures.

MANN, ALFRED. *The Study of Fugue,* Rutgers University Press, New Brunswick, New Jersey, 1958. English translations of some of the Baroque and Classical texts on counterpoint and fugue along with commentaries make this informative supplementary reading, particularly since it gives us an insight into the type of training the great composers of the past had.

OLDROYD, GEORGE. *The Technique and Spirit of Fugue,* Oxford University Press, London, New York, and Toronto, 1948. This text is written from the standpoint of the composer of a fugue. Each chapter discusses the problems and choices confronting the composer at every stage of fugal writing. Especially helpful are the chapters on "The Lay-Out of a Fugue," "Observations Concerning Fugue Subjects" (showing the harmonic implications of the subject), "The Codetta — Its Importance and Potentiality," and the final chapter, "A Course of Study."

PISTON, WALTER. *Counterpoint,* W. W. Norton and Company, New York, 1947. Certain chapters serve well as a preliminary study for both fugue and invention, especially those entitled "The Melodic Curve," "Melodic Rhythm," "The Harmonic Basis," and "Motive Structure." The chapter on "Invertible Counterpoint" is one of the best and most thorough descriptions of this technique extant, and might be used in conjunction with Chapter III and Chapter XVI of this book, especially during the study of fugues with one or two counter-subjects and inventions using double or triple counterpoint. Since canon plays an important part in fugue (episodes, sequences, and stretto) and in invention, Chapters X and XI in Piston's book might serve as useful supplementary reading.

PROUT, EBENEZER. *Fugue,* Augener, London, 1891. This is still one of the great texts on fugue, rich in examples and in insights. The chapters on "Subject," "Answer," "Exposition," and "Stretto" are exhaustive and well illustrated. Certain chapters contain extensive material on unusual aspects of fugue, namely the chapters entitled "Fughetta and Fugato," "Fugues on More Than One Subject," "The Fugue on a Choral," and "Accompanied Fugue."

———. *Double Counterpoint and Canon,* Augener, London, 1891. This is an extremely valuable and exhaustive treatment of contrapuntal inversion, not only at the 15th, 10th, and 12th but at rarer intervals. In the chapter entitled "Double-Counterpoint at the Rarer Intervals," Prout gives tables showing how intervals invert at the 9th, 11th, 13th, and 14th as well as numerous examples of these inversions. Other chapters which are pertinent to the present study are entitled "Triple Counterpoint and Quadruple Counterpoint," "Imitation," "Two-Part Canon," and "Curiosities of Canon."

RUBBRA, EDMUND. *Counterpoint,* Hutchinson University Library, London, 1960. This little book contains much philosophy and many insights on the nature of counterpoint, canon, fugue, and other contrapuntal forms, and is of especial use as background reading to reveal directions taken in contrapuntal writing over the past four and a half centuries. Some especially valuable remarks on twentieth-century counterpoint are contained in the chapters on "Fugue" and "Free Counterpoint."

SEARLE, HUMPHREY. *Twentieth Century Counterpoint,* John de Graff, New York, 1954. An informative survey of newer contrapuntal techniques. Of special interest are a group of chapters devoted to individual composers, describing their unique contrapuntal characteristics, Stravinsky, Milhaud, Bartók, Hindemith, and Schoenberg.

TOVEY, DONALD. *The Forms of Music,* Meridian Books, Cleveland, Ohio, 1945. This selection from the writings of Tovey contains several chapters of general interest to students of fugue and invention, notably those entitled "Contrapuntal Forms," "Counterpoint," and "Fugue."

# List of Musical Examples

# Index